Classic Gollies

TO KNIT, SEW & CROCHET

Classic Gollies

TO KNIT, SEW & CROCHET

Marjory Fainges

Kangaroo Press

This book is dedicated to my mother Mrs Florence Ratcliffe of Toowoomba, who is now 92, for the time she spent teaching me how to knit, and overseeing my first laborious attempts at making a Golly over 55 years ago, and giving me a love of these delightful aspects of childhood.

Acknowledgments

My sincere thanks go to all those who have helped me in any way in compiling this book on Gollies. To Jacki Brooks who I have known for many years who so graciously gave of her time to write the Foreword, to Shirleyanne McKay (NSW) and Ross Schmidt (WA) who have over the years sent me lovely old patterns, to Barbara Brooks (Maryborough, Qld), a real Golly lover who so willingly helped proof many of the Gollies at short notice, to Coats Patons who have kindly given me permission to update their old patterns, to my daughter-in-law Beth Fainges who helped with the Wallhanging, to my wonderful husband and friend of over 45 years for his help drawing the patterns and making some of the wonderful miniature props, to Ruth Stahl (USA) who kindled the flame once again in regard to my love of Gollies, and to all those people whose encouragements helped me to finish the book.

CLASSIC GOLLIES TO KNIT, SEW & CHROCHET

First published in Australia in 1998 by Kangaroo Press
an imprint of Simon & Schuster (Australia) Pty Limited
20 Barcoo Street, East Roseville NSW 2069

A Viacom Company
Sydney New York London Toronto Tokyo Singapore

National Library of Australia
Cataloguing-in-Publication data

Fainges, Marjory, 1933–

Classic gollies to knit, sew & crochet

Includes index
ISBN 0 86417 940 5
1. Soft toy making — Patterns. I. Title

745.5924

Set in Goudy OlSt BT 10/12
Goudy HandTooled BT

Printed through Colorcraft Ltd., Hong Kong

10 9 8 7 6 5

Contents

Foreword

HAPPILY THE HISTORY and beginnings of the Golliwogg are not as obscure as the Teddy's, for we do know who actually made and named the first Golli—Florence Upton.

Florence Upton was born in New York of English parents in 1873, and returned with her mother to live in England at the age of 16 after her father died. Florence took with her to England a strange black doll that she named Golliwogg.

At age 22, Florence's first Golliwogg book was published. There had been difficulties in finding a publisher for the very different nurseryland character. Eventually Longmans, Green and Company of London and New York published the first Golliwogg book, which proved a huge success.

In all, thirteen Golliwogg books were published, the first in 1895—almost one a year, with Florence's mother Bertha Upton writing the verse and her very talented daughter illustrating the books. The books and publication dates are:

The Adventures of Two Dutch Dolls—and a Golliwogg, c.1895
The Golliwogg's Bicycle Club, c.1896
The Golliwogg at the Sea-Side, c.1898
The Golliwogg in War, c.1899
The Golliwogg's Polar Adventures, c.1900
The Golliwogg's Auto-Go-Cart, c.1901
The Golliwogg's Air-Ship, c.1902
The Golliwogg's Circus, c.1903
The Golliwogg in Holland, c.1904
The Golliwogg's Fox-Hunt, c.1905
The Golliwogg's Desert Island, c.1906
The Golliwogg's Christmas, c.1907
The Golliwogg in the African Jungle, c.1909

Miss Upton was a very talented and prolific artist, illustrating other books, contributing to magazines and holding her own art exhibitions.

The origin of the name 'Golliwogg' is not cut and dried, and has as many variations as the origins given for the name 'Teddy Bear'. One story is that the name derived from the W.O.G. armbands worn by the Egyptian workers in British-occupied Alexandria—W.O.G. standing for 'Working on Government Services'. The workers were *ghuls*, so perhaps the *ghul*-W.O.G. became Golliwogg.

According to Pollock's *Dictionary of English Dolls*, the preserve-making company of Robertsons, who use the Golliwogg as their trademark, put forward another theory, that the name originated from 'polliwog', an old-fashioned term for tadpole. Ah well. He is Golliwogg, and no other name would have been just right!

The Golliwogg's history has not been without controversy—poor old Golli suffered being 'banned' during the 1960s by British Race Relations officers, who declared that the image of the Golliwogg was 'insulting and offensive to the black people'. Enid Blyton's *Noddy* children's books were banned because of the mischievous Golliwogg.

The sales of the Golliwogg dropped drastically and in 1966 the British toymaking firm of Dean's produced two white Golliwoggs, 'Mr Smith Senior', 43 cm (17"), and 'Mr Smith Junior', 33 cm (13"). Made from white sailcloth, these toys wore a striped shirt, a vest and a bow tie. They had cloth button eyes and dark plush hair. These white gollies didn't prove a success and production ceased within the year.

Not even the efforts of the Race Relations officers could keep the Golliwogg down, however. Public opinion, from all groups of people, demanded the return of the lovable rascal. In 1982 Britain's *Daily Mail*, in an article by John Hampshire, reported: 'Golly, back in style'. London department stores soon had Golliwogg back on their shelves and selling up a storm!

Although Golliwogg is always considered to be an English toy, the US influence is undeniable. The Dutch dolls who are Golliwogg's constant companions in the Golliwogg books are dressed in the stars and stripes of the US flag. The costume that Golliwogg wears is also very like the costumes of the early US black minstrels; perhaps this influenced Florence when she dressed her Golliwogg.

Many companies in both England and Australia produced Golliwoggs commercially, and these are very collectable today. However, the very nature of Golli's structure made him a wonderful toy to reproduce at home if there was no money for a shop-bought toy. There was always an old jumper to unpick and knit up into a 'new' Golli, or Mum's rag bag held all the materials required to produce a wonderful cloth Golli. These sometimes unlovely home-made toys, made with more love than skill, are also now very collectable, treasured mementos of a long-gone childhood.

And now these rare and treasured early patterns are reproduced here for Golli lovers to make themselves at home. Enjoy.

Jacki Brooks

(Jacki Brooks is Executive Editor of Doll Digest Publications, publishers of *Doll Digest* and *Bear Facts Review*. A collector and historian of Golliwoggs for well over twenty years, Jacki includes articles on Golliwoggs in both magazines and is thrilled at Golli's renewed popularity.)

Introduction

Over one hundred years ago Miss Florence Upton wrote and illustrated a series of children's books featuring the antics of a wooden doll and her friend Golliwogg. Ever since then children, first in the English-speaking world and later world-wide, have been fascinated by the loveable dolls that have been created in the image of the character now known as Golly. With his black face, stand-up black hair, large eyes and cheeky grin, dressed in bright colours, he has been the companion and confidante of many a child during the last century, at times equalling the power of the other famous soft toy of childhood—the Teddy Bear.

All my five children had Gollies knitted for them when they were babies by their paternal grandmother. As each child got older, their much-loved Gollies, through being carted around by the arm or leg, 'grew' these particular parts of their anatomy much longer—to the point where at least two of my sons had a competition to see who could tie their poor Golly's arms or legs in a knot. Happily these favourite toys survived, and kept their cheeky grins, till the boys had well and truly outgrown them, but the children still have very happy memories of their beloved Gollies.

In this book I aim to give you the chance to create your own Golly, or a gift for a favourite child, in whichever medium you are happiest working in, whether it be knitting, crochet, or sewing. Along the way I have included a few extra ideas using the Golly persona, such as a teacosy for your favourite teapot, decorating a pair of children's shoes or slippers, a hand or glove puppet for a child to use its imagination and to while away the hours, and even a baby's bib.

This way, yet another generation can love, hug and enjoy this loveable character once again.

About these patterns

In this book I recreate various aspects of Gollie's past. For example, Ozzie Golly has a round nose, as did many of the German-made Gollies in the early years of this century. Four of the patterns are for Gollies similar to those made during the years of the Second World War, when instructions and patterns for toys that could be made at home from scraps of wool or fabric were given in many of the women's magazines and knitting booklets.

A small version of a Golly pattern designed by Joy Toys during the war years has also been included—he has been given a triangular felt nose, another form of Golly nose depicted in many children's books in years past.

Materials & Techniques

Wool and fabrics For the large knitted and crocheted Gollies I have used 8-ply wool, for the smaller ones 4-ply, but it is really up to you what wool or yarn you use. By changing the ply (or denier) of the material you are using in conjunction with the size of the knitting needle or crochet hook, you can make the Golly of your choice in any size you wish—large or small.

For the sewn Gollies I have used either black velvet or black felt for the famous black Golly face hands and feet, but any black cotton fabric can be used. Following the practice set many years ago, in many cases the Gollies have their clothes sewn as part of the body. Some have separate trousers, and these can be made in the fabric of your choice—cotton or velvet, striped, checked or plain. Their jackets can be made in either fabric or felt, but if you use fabric you will have to face the lapels on their famous jackets. And of course you must finish off your Golly's outfit with his most famous trademark—the bow tie at the neck.

Stuffing While some people stuff a toy quite firmly (which on the whole I have done for the Gollies shown here), others prefer a much softer look. This is entirely up to you the creator, but be aware that the form and firmness of the stuffing may affect the fit of the clothing, for example the length of trouser legs, so it is wise to check before you cut out pattern pieces when your Golly wears separate clothing. The Dacron offcuts available in large bags from many outlets, which must be teased slightly and then used in smaller pieces, give a lovely firm finish if used correctly. If you prefer to use the small bags of Dacron stuffing available from fabric and craft stores, you will find it is quite soft, and you will use a lot more of this to get a firm finish.

Colour Golly was always made of black material, relying on the colours of his outfit to give him that individual appeal to children that has lasted over the years.

As the original Golly was male, the colours traditionally used to dress him were red for his jacket and blue for his trousers—sometimes this colour scheme was reversed—but in this day and age, any combination of colours can be used to give a bright fun finish to your creation. In later years some female Gollies were made with striped skirts, but these innovations never reached the popularity of the old, traditional style Golly.

Hair variations When it comes to giving your Golly his famous hairstyle, it is up to you what type of hair you wish to give him. The easiest of them all is to use one of the many black faux fur fabrics that are now available through various craft and teddy outlets—a medium to short fur fabric gives the best result. For the tiny Gollies I used the old method of winding wool round a large knitting needle. The famous curls of some of the knitted Gollies were knitted as part of the pattern—try this method if you can, it does give excellent results. Some even had their hair made by what is known as the 'knotting' method. Both were favourite methods used in days gone by—but if you can't master the techniques, or don't have the time to spend on these two applications (they do take time to achieve) use the faux fur. For one of the wartime Gollies I followed the method that was used on the original—a length of felt 'fringed' produced the famous standup hair.

Glue As many of the Gollies' eyes and mouths are made from felt, usually glued onto the face, select a good quick clear-drying craft glue.

Australian glues which I have found successful include:

- Sullivan's Craft Glue, available from many of the Crazy Clarks, Dollar and Sense type of stores now found throughout Australia, for around $2.
- Craft Smart Craft Glue, available from many of the larger chain stores and craft shops, e.g. Spotlight.

Eyes With what, and how, you portray the famous black and white eyes of a Golly is entirely up to you. You can use any of the methods given in the book, from the simple white sequin and bead eyes of the small Gollies to the modern sew-on or glue-on plastic googly moving eyes sold in craft shops, large supermarkets or department stores to the tremendous variety of eyes possible by using white and black felt either glued or sewn to the face, or a combination of white felt backs with slightly domed black buttons. Just by changing the eyes each Golly will look different.

Mouth Another way of giving your Golly his very own individuality. He can have a mouth sewn from wool, or made in a variety of shapes in felt or velvet (either one or two pieces)—perhaps the 'watermelon' mouth, or even the wide round open mouth to give that surprised look.

Hints on using felt As many of the Golly patterns use felt in bodies or clothes, here are a couple of hints to help you get the best results. Felt is an excellent medium to work in, once you come to terms with it. If you are sewing by hand, you can work on the piece anywhere, even while watching television.

1. When buying felt always 'tweak' a corner to see if it stretches. If the felt stretches quite a bit in one direction don't buy, as the finished article will overstretch and you will not get the shape you are aiming for.
2. It is a good idea to steam iron all felt before you use it. It gives the felt a better finish and helps reduce the possibility of overstretching from uneven stuffing.
3. Wherever possible oversew the seams. (Use your thumbnail as a sewing guide.) Use small even stitches to keep the seam even. When the work is turned right side out, it will look as though the seam has been machine sewn.

Important If you are making any of the Gollies featured in this book for a young child (under 3 years), care should be taken to always use well glued on felt or fabric eyes, or carefully and well sewn on plastic eyes. Do not use sequin or bead eyes on a Golly you intend to give to young children, as they can be plucked off by little fingers and swallowed if not glued on securely.

Source of Materials

Wool or Yarn Available from any large department stores, or Big W, Target, Kmart, Spotlight, craft shops and specialty stores.
Felt Spotlight and most craft shops
Eyes Most craft shops

Bendigo Woollen Mills
Lansall St, Bendigo Victoria 3550
Phone: (03) 5442 2918
Fax: (03) 5442 2918
Mail order service
Credit cards accepted

Champion Textiles
16–18 O'Connell St, Newtown NSW 2042
Phone: (02) 9519 6677
Fax: (02) 9517 9605
Mail order service
Credit cards accepted

Useful Information

Wool thicknesses

Australian	*American*
2-ply	2-ply fingering
3-ply	3-ply fingering
4-ply	4-ply fingering
5-ply	

Knitting needle sizes

Metric (mm)	*Imperial*	*American*
2.0	14	0
2.5	13–12	1
3.0	11	2–3
3.5	10	4
3.75	9	5
4.0	8	6
4.5	7	7
5.0	6	8
5.5	5	9
6.0	4	10
6.5	3	—
7.0	2	10½
7.5	1	—

Crochet hooks

Metric (mm)	*Imperial*	*American*
2.0	14	B/1
2.5	12	C/2
3.0	10	D/3
3.5	9	E/4
4.0	8	F/5
4.5	7	G/6
5.0	6	H/8
5.5	5	I/9
6.0	4	J/10
7.0	2	—

Abbreviations and terminology

* *	repeat instructions between * *
****	refer back to previous section of pattern
alt	alternate
beg	beginning
C	contrast, or lesser colour used in 2-colour knitting
dec	decrease
g	gram/s
garter st	work every row in knit stitch
inc	work twice into st to make 2 sts
in	inch(es)
k	knit
m1	make a st by placing wool over needle before next st
MC	main colour used in 2-colour knitting
mm	millimetre(s)
m st	moss stitch—work k1, p1, alternately in following rows to give a broken rib effect; usually worked on an uneven no. of sts
no.	number
oz	ounce(s)
p	purl
psso	pass slipped st over
rep	repeat
rib	usually either k1, p1, or k2, p2, normally worked on an even no. of sts, repeated to end of row
rib	in the case of garter st, the number of raised rows showing on one side of knitting
sl or sl st	slip the st onto needle
st(s)	stitch(es)
st st	stocking st—working one row in knit st and following row in purl st
tbl	through back of loop
tog	work 2 sts together to form 1 st
turn	reverse the way of knitting by working back on the needle just worked
wl fwd	bringing wool to front of work before working next st, thus making a st; used in patterns and for small buttonholes

Handy hints

1. Knit through back of stitch on all cast-on stitches, using the two-needle method, to give a firm edge, particularly when this method has been used to make a buttonhole.
2. When picking up a stitch, pick up and knit before transferring it onto other needle.

Equivalent crochet terms

Australian/European	*American*
ch (chain)	= ch (chain)
st st (single crochet)	= sl st (slip stitch)
dc (double crochet)	= sc (single crochet)
tr (treble)	= dc (double crochet)

Tension

As some knitters work more loosely or tightly than others, I suggest you work a trial piece of knitting, say 10 stitches by 10 rows, to see if you are using the tension recommended in the pattern.

If your sample has more stitches or rows than in the pattern, use needles a size smaller; use needles a size larger if your sample has less stitches or rows. If you are an uneven knitter here is a little hint—knit your purl rows using a size larger needle than in your knit rows. It works.

Knitted Gollies

Teeny Tiny Golly

Illustrated on page 17

This lovely little 14 cm (5½") Golly can be used as a brooch or even as an occupant of a dollshouse. I have based this design on the character Golly from the Betty & Golly *series of adventures, very popular in many of the children's comics and annuals published in England in the 1930s and 1940s. This Golly was always depicted wearing a simple top and trousers, finished with a wide collar and with two buttons at the waist. He is quick to knit in 4-ply, with his clothing made in two colours, with just a touch of white in his collar.*

Materials

25 g (1 oz) 4-ply wool in black
25 g (1 oz) 4-ply wool in red or chosen colour for pants
25 g (1 oz) 4-ply wool in yellow or chosen colour for jumper
small ball 4-ply wool in white for collar
(these quantities will make several Gollies)
1 pair 2.75 mm (12) [US 2] knitting needles
1 large 6 mm or 7 mm (4 or 6) [US 10 or 10½] knitting needle to make the hair
4 medium gold sequins for buttons
2 small white sequins for eyes
2 small black beads for pupils for eyes
length of red embroidery cotton for mouth

Tension

8 sts over 2.5 cm (1") width

Legs (make 2)

Using black wool and 2.75 mm (12) [US 2] needles, cast on 4 sts.
1st row: Knit
2nd row: Knit, inc at each end of needle (6 sts).
Work 4 rows in garter st. Break off black.
Join in trouser colour.
1st row: Knit, inc 1 st at both ends of needle (8 sts).
Starting with a purl row, work 15 rows in st st. Break off yarn.
Push these sts to end of needle, and make another foot and leg in the same manner.

Body (make 2)

Continuing with trouser colour, knit the 7 sts of 2nd leg, then knit last st of second leg, and 1st st of first leg tog, then knit 7 sts of first leg (14 sts).
Work 7 rows in st st, starting with a purl row. Break off trouser colour, join in jumper colour.
Work 13 rows in garter st.
Cast off 3 sts at beginning of the next 2 rows (8 sts). Cast off.
Make another piece in the same way.

Arms (make 2)

Using black wool cast on 8 sts for hand, and knit 5 rows.
Break off black and join in jumper colour
1st row: Knit, inc 1 st at each end of needle (10 sts).
Knit 5 rows in garter st.
Inc 1 st at each end of next row, then knit 4 rows in garter st.
Cast off 2 sts at beginning of next 2 rows.
Knit 1 row.
Next row: k2 tog at beg and end of row. Cast off.
Sew arms to body at armholes, beginning and ending at 3rd garter st rib from waist.
Sew up sleeve seams, and then side seams of jumper and rest of body. Stuff body and arms, stuffing the armhole area less firmly than the rest, so that arm movement is more flexible.

Head (make 2)

Using black wool cast on 6 sts.
1st row: Knit.
2nd row: Purl.
3rd row: Inc 1 st at each end of knit row.
Next 3 rows: St st.
Repeat the last 4 rows.
Dec 1 st at each end of the next row, then knit one row (8 sts).
Repeat last two rows once, then cast off for top of head.
Sew two pieces of head together, leaving cast-on edge open.

Stuff firmly, being careful not to stretch stitches so that stuffing shows. Carefully sew head to body, stuffing either piece a little more as you go if necessary to make the neck area stronger.

Collar

With white wool, cast on 20 sts.
1st row: Knit.
2nd row: Inc in 1st st, knit to last 2 st, inc in next st, k1.
Repeat the last two rows twice. Cast off.
Sew collar in position around neck.

Hair

Thread a darning needle with a length of wool, and wind the end of the wool 6–8 times around the large knitting needle; slip darning needle twice through windings around knitting needle, pull up, slip rings (now curls) off knitting needle, and darn curls into position on head. Repeat until you have curls going from just above where his ear might be on one side over the top to the other side.

Finish off by sewing two gold sequins at the waist (front and back) for buttons.

Whee Golly

Illustrated on page 17

Just the right size to fit in a pocket, or to become a toy for your favourite doll or bear, this 15 cm (6") Golly is quick to knit and simple to make. Although he looks as though he is wearing a separate jacket, this is a clever illusion, and very easy to do.

Materials

50 g (2 oz) ball of 8-ply black wool
50 g (2 oz) ball of 8-ply blue wool
50 g (2 oz) ball of 8-ply red wool
50 g (2 oz) ball of 8-ply yellow wool
(these quantities will make several Gollies)
1 pair of 3.25 mm (10) [US 3] knitting needles
small amount of dacron stuffing
4 gold beads
2 large white sequins and 2 small black sequins or beads or sew-on eyes

Tension

8 sts over 2.5 cm (1") width

1st leg

Starting at base of first leg, with blue wool, cast on 7 sts.
Work 18 rows in st st.
Leave these sts on a separate needle (or knitting safety holder) until needed**. Break off wool.

2nd leg

Work second leg as for first leg to **, knit one row, then work across the 7 sts of the first leg (14 sts).

Body

Work 7 rows in st st on the 14 sts of the legs, starting with a purl row.
Break off blue wool. Join in yellow wool.
Work 12 rows in st st, starting with a knit row.
Dec 1 st at both ends of the next 2 rows (10 sts).
Break off yellow***.
Join in black wool.
Working in st st, inc 1 st at both ends of the next 3 rows (16 sts).
Work 11 rows in st st.

Hair

1st row: *Insert the point of the right-hand needle into the next st on left-hand needle, then wind the yarn 3 times over the first finger of left hand, taking the wool over the point of the right-hand needle each time. Then draw the 3 made loops through the st on the left-hand needle, slip these loops onto the point of the left hand needle, and knit all the loops tog with the original st on the left-hand needle in the usual way. Gently pull the loops so that they fasten, before working the next sts*. Repeat from * to * until 1 st remains, k1 (16 sts).
2nd row: Purl.
Repeat the last 2 rows 3 times.
Work 11 rows in st st. Cast off.

Work another body piece to ***. Cast off.
Sew base of cast-off section of head of first body piece to cast-off neck of second body piece.
You will notice that the loops of hair fall down further on the first few rows of hair, so make that the back of your Golly when sewing him up. You may have to take a needle threaded double with black yarn, and carefully darn across the stitches at the base of the hairline at the top portion of the face for a good finish, due to the way the special loops have been worked.
Sew both sides of the head together to the base of the head.

Sleeves and hands (make 2)

Beginning with the hands, cast on 10 sts with black wool.
Work 2 rows in st st.
Break off black wool and join in red wool.
Work 6 rows in st st.
Inc 1 st at both ends of the next row, and following 6th row (14 sts).
Work 2 rows in st st.
Dec 1 st at both ends of the next 5 rows (4 sts). Cast off.
Work another sleeve and hand the same.

To make up body

Sew the two shoulder seams, then, folding each sleeve in half, match the top centre of each sleeve to the end of the shoulder seams, and sew in place down both sides of yellow part of body to within 5 rows of blue pants. Sew up remaining side seams of yellow bodice, red sleeves and black hands, sewing across the end of the arms.
Carefully stuff head and arms.
Sew both the side seams and inner leg seams of blue trousers, but do not sew up bottom of each trouser leg.
Stuff the rest of the body and the legs.

Shoes (make 4 pieces)

Using either yellow or black yarn, cast on 4 sts.
Work 2 rows in st st.
Continuing in st st, inc 1 st at both ends of the next rows (6 sts).
Work 3 rows in st st.
Dec 1 st at both ends of the following row (4 sts).
Work 1 row. Cast off.
Sew two pieces together at the narrow end, wrong sides facing, leaving the fatter end open. Stuff. Place open part of shoe up against bottom of leg, and carefully sew around the base of leg and shoe, stuffing the last part before finally sewing up.
If the base of the shoe is firmly but flatly stuffed, the little Golly will be able to stand erect against a support.

Coat

The 2 fronts and back of the coat are worked in one—the arms of the Golly form part of the coat.
Using red wool, cast on 40 sts (bottom of back).
Work 12 rows in st st.

Armholes

Divide the sts for the fronts and back.
Row 13: k10 for right front, turn (place the remaining 30 sts on a spare needle or holder).
Row 14: Purl.
Row 15: k1, p1, knit to last 2 sts, k2 tog.
Row 16: p2 tog, purl to last st, k1.
Row 17: k1, p1, k1, p1, knit to last 2 st, k2 tog (7 sts).
Row 18: *k1, p1*, repeat from * to * twice, k1. Cast off in moss st.

Back

Rejoin wool to the right side of the remaining 30 sts, k20, turn (leave last 10 sts on a spare needle or holder).
Row 14: Purl.
Row 15: k2 tog, knit to last 2 sts, k2 tog.
Row 16: p2 tog, purl to last 2 sts, p2 tog.
Repeat 15th and 16th rows once.
Cast off remaining 12 sts.

Left front

Rejoin wool and knit 1 row on the remaining 10 sts.
Row 14: Purl.
Row 15: k2 tog, knit to the last 2 sts, p1, k1.
Row 16: k1, purl to last 2 sts, p2 tog.
Row 17: k2 tog, knit to last 4 sts, p1, k1, p1, k1.
Row 18: *k1, p1*, repeat from * to * to last st, k1. Cast off in moss st.
Sew up side seams of jacket and place jacket in position on Golly, matching armholes with top of arms. Using red wool, carefully sew jacket to body arms, to form the sleeves of the jacket. Sew the top of the back of the jacket to the top of the back body. Turn back the moss stitch lapels of jacket and catch with a tiny thread.
Trim jacket with gold beads down both fronts.

Bow

With blue wool cast on 5 sts.
Work 2 rows in moss st.
Next row: Working in moss st, dec 1 st at both ends of row.
Work 2 rows in moss st. Cast off.
Sew bow at base of neck.

Face

Embroider eyes using white and black wool, or use special sew-on eyes, or use 1 large white and one small black sequin per eye.
Sew a happy mouth in red wool.

Beau Golly

Illustrated on page 18

This rather jazzy Golly, 40 cm (16") tall, complete in his lovely formal coat, bow tie, and cheeky expression, just asks to be made. Adapted from an old Patons pattern, he takes just a little more effort than some of the other Gollies, but he is well worth it.

Materials

75 g (3 oz) of 8-ply wool in dark blue or chosen colour for trousers
75 g (3 oz) of 8-ply wool in red or chosen colour for jacket
50 g (2 oz) of black 8-ply wool for head, hands and shoes
25 g (1 oz) of 8-ply wool in white or chosen colour for vest
1 pair of 4 mm (8) [US 6] knitting needles
1 pair of 3 mm (11) [US 3] knitting needles
1 pair of 2.75 mm (12) [US 2] knitting needles
4 gold buttons for decoration
2 sew-on or glue-on plastic googly eyes
small piece of red felt or velvet for mouth
length of black fur fabric 5 cm (2") wide (if you have trouble working hair as directed)

Tension

6 sts over 2.5 cm (1") width

Body and legs

Starting with the legs:
Using the colour chosen for the trousers and 4 mm (8) [US 6] knitting needles, cast on 17 sts.
Work 54 rows in st st for 1st leg. Break off wool.
On the same needle, cast on another 17 sts and work 54 rows in st st. You now have 34 sts on the one needle. Proceed as follows:
1st row: Knit across both sets of sts.
2nd row: Purl.
3rd row: k2 tog, knit to last 2 sts, k2 tog.
4th row: Purl.
5th row: Knit.
6th row: Purl.
Repeat the last 4 rows twice (28 sts).
Break off trouser colour and join in jacket colour.
Work 30 rows in garter st.
Cast off 3 sts at beg of next 4 rows for shoulders.
Cast off remaining sts.

Jacket tails (make two)

Using jacket colour and 4 mm (8) [US 6] needles, cast on 30 sts.
1st row: Knit.
2nd row: k2 tog, knit to end of row.
Repeat 1st and 2nd rows until 3 sts remain, k3 tog. Cast off.

Arms and hands (make 2)

With black wool and 2.75 mm (12) [US 2] needles, cast on 24 sts.
1st row: Knit.
2nd row: Purl.
3rd row: Inc once in 1st st, k10, inc once in next 2 sts, k10, inc once in last st (28 sts).
Work 7 rows in st st, beginning with a purl row.
Next row: k2 tog, k10, (k2 tog) twice, k10, k2 tog.
Next row: Purl. Break off black wool.
Using 3 mm (11) [US 3] needles and white wool, proceed as follows:
Work 6 rows in st st. Break off white.
Join in colour of jacket and work as follows:
Work 36 rows in garter st.
Next row: Inc once in 1st st, knit to last st, inc once in last st.
Work 5 rows in garter st. Cast off.

Vest

Using white wool (or colour of your choice) and 3 mm (11) [US 3] needles, cast on 2 sts.
1st row: Knit.
Work 4 rows in garter st, inc. once at each end of needle in 1st row.
Repeat from ** to ** 6 times. Cast off.

Right lapel

Using trouser colour and 3 mm (11) [US 3] needles, cast on 5 sts.

Left: The original GOLLIWOGG, with his companions Peggy and Sarah Jane, is housed at Chequers, the British Prime Minister's country residence

Below: TEENY TINY GOLLY is a lovely little 14 cm (5½") fellow knitted in 4-ply, just the right size to go in a dollshouse or be worn as a brooch. He is taking his brand new bike to show his mate next door (page 12)

Left: WHEE GOLLY, just 15 cm (6") tall and knitted in 8-ply, is so happy to have sold all the day's fruit and vegetables from his nice new fruit barrow, made to one-twelfth scale by my husband Jim, that he's taking his pet bear for a ride (page 14)

Above: BEAU GOLLY tries to see the whole of his 40 cm (16") as he peeks in the mirror of a one-sixth scale version of a 1920s wooden dressing table to see if his wonderful striped bow tie is sitting right. Who could resist him? (page 16)
Right: BEAU GOLLY (detail)

** *1st row:* Knit
Repeat 1st row twice.
4th row: Inc once in first st, knit to last st, inc once in last st.
Repeat last 4 rows once.
Work 9 rows in garter st, inc once at each end of needle in the last row.
Repeat last 9 rows twice.
Work 2 rows in garter st. Cast off**.

Left lapel

With trouser colour and 3 mm (11) [US 3] needles, cast on 2 sts.
1st and 2nd rows: Knit.
Work 4 rows in garter st, inc once at each end of the needle in 1st row.
Repeat last 4 rows once.
Work as right lapel from ** to **.

Bow tie

Using 3 mm (11) [US 3] needles, cast on 16 sts in the first colour (red).
1st row: Knit (in first colour).
2nd and 3rd rows: Knit in second colour (white).
4th and 5th rows: Knit in first colour.
Repeat the last 4 rows until 42 rows have been worked.
Work 1 row in first colour. Cast off in first colour (red).
Sew two lines of gathering thread at middle and draw up tight. End off.
Sew bow in position at base of neck.

Shoes (make two)

With black wool and 4 mm (8) [US 6] knitting needles, cast on 28 sts.
1st row: Knit.
2nd row: k11, inc in next st, k3, inc, k12.
3rd row: Knit.
4th row: k12, inc, k3, inc, k13.
5th row: Knit.
6th row: k13, inc, k3, inc, k14.
7th row: Knit.
8th row: k14, inc, k3, inc, k15.
9th row: Knit. Cast off.

Head

With black wool and 2.75 mm (12) [US 2] needles, cast on 19 sts.
1st row: Knit.
2nd row: Inc once in 1st st, purl to last st, inc in last st.
Repeat 1st and 2nd rows twice.
Work 6 rows straight in st st.
Next row: Inc once in first st, knit to last st, inc once in last st.
Work 17 rows straight in st st.
Next row: k2 tog, knit to last 2 sts, k2 tog.
Work 3 rows in st st.
Next row: k2 tog, knit to last 2 sts, k2 tog. Cast off.

Neck

Using white wool (or colour chosen for vest) and 4 mm (8) [US 6] needles, cast on 34 sts.
Work 8 rows in garter st. Cast off.

Hair

Using black wool and 4 mm (8) [US 6] needles, cast on 39 sts.
1st row: k1, *insert needle knitways in next st, place your forefinger at back of st, then wind yarn anti-clockwise around needle and finger twice, then round point of needle again, draw loops through sts on left hand needle, slip these back onto left hand needle and knit all loops tbl as one st, repeat from * to last st, k1.
2nd row: Knit.
Repeat the last 2 rows. Cast off.

To make up

Join both halves of body together at shoulder, leaving neck open. Sew top of arms to armholes, beginning and ending at 5th rib of garter st from waistline of jacket. Sew up sleeve and hand seams, and also the side seams of jacket and trousers, leaving bottom edge of trousers open.

Sew up shoes, leaving top open, stuff firmly, and sew to bottom of legs, point of shoe facing to the front.

Stuff legs and bottom of body firmly, then stuff arms, but leaving a small gap in the stuffing at armhole seams so that arms can move; stuff rest of body to neck.

Join both halves of head together leaving neck portion open. Stuff firmly.

Join the two side edges of neck, then join the cast-off edge of neck around neck opening on body. Stuff neck very firmly, then sew neck opening onto head around top edge of neck, if necessary adding extra stuffing as you go to make the neck area firm.

Pin hair piece in position on top of head, and sew to head firmly.

Sew vest to centre front of body with cast-off edge along neckline.

Pin lapels in place at side of vest, folding straight edges towards front, sew in place, and fold back into position. Trim lapel with a gold button. If you wish you can sew button through lapel to jacket to hold lapels in place.

With long end of jacket tails to the top, pin so that the straight edges of jacket tails face each other at middle of back, then pin long cast-on edge around waist into position at front, near lapels.

Sew a matching gold button on each side of back, just above tail split.

Finally sew on eyes, and glue mouth into position with clear-drying craft glue.

Ozzie Golly

Illustrated on page 35

Although my Ozzie is made in Australia's traditional colours of green and golden yellow, he can be made in any colours of your choice. This 36 cm (14") Golly would make an excellent sporting mascot as well as an ideal toy.
Many of the drawings and illustrations to be found in old children's books and annuals feature Gollies sporting either a triangular-shaped nose or a separate round or button nose. Ozzie has been made in this older tradition, with a small round nose added after making up, but you can leave it off if you prefer.

Materials

50 g (2 oz) ball of black 8-ply wool
50 g (2 oz) ball of main colour 8-ply wool
50 g (2 oz) ball of contrast colour 8-ply wool
1 pair of 3.25 mm (10) [US 3] knitting needles
3 mm (10) [US D/3] crochet hook
5 gold buttons
scraps of black and white felt for the eyes or 2 plastic sew-on googly eyes
5 cm (2") length of black faux fur for hair
50 cm (20") of bright ribbon

Tension

7 sts over 2.5 cm (1") width

Body back

Using black yarn, start at the lower edge of one leg by casting on 16 stitches.
1st row: Knit.
2nd row: Purl.
Repeat these two rows once. Break off black.
Change to main colour and work 40 rows in st st.
Next row: Inc once in first st, knit to end of row.
Next row: Purl.
Repeat the last 2 rows once.
Break off wool and leave these sts on a spare needle.
Work another leg in the same way, but working the increase sts at the opposite end of the needle.
Slip the two legs onto one needle, with the inc section in the middle and the straight edges on the outside.
With right side of work facing, work as follows:
Next row: k16, inc once in next st, k2, inc once in next st, k16 (38 sts).
Next row: p16, inc once in next st purlwise, p4, inc once in next st purlwise, p16 (40 sts).
Work 4 rows in st st without shaping.
Next row: k2 tog, knit to last 2 sts, k2 tog.
Work 3 rows in st st without shaping.
Repeat the last 4 rows once.
Work 2 sts tog at each end of needle in the next 4 rows (28 sts).
Next row: (k2 tog, k2) three times, (k2 tog) twice, (k2, k2 tog) three times (20 sts).
Next row: Purl.
**Break off main colour, and join in contrast colour.
1st row: Inc in first st, knit to last st, inc.
2nd row: Knit.
Repeat the last 2 rows twice (26 sts).
Work 6 rows in garter st without shaping.

Arms

Cast on 20 sts at the beginning of the next 2 rows (66 sts).
Work 13 rows in garter st without shaping.
Next row: Cast off 25 sts. Knit to end of row.
Repeat the last row once (16 sts remain).
Break off contrast colour, join in black.

Head

With right side of work facing, on the remaining 16 sts work as follows:
****1st row:* Knit.
2nd row: Purl.
3rd row: Knit.

4th row: Inc once in the next 2 sts, purl to last 2 sts, inc once in each st.
5th row: Inc once in 1st st, knit to last st, inc in last st.
6th row: Inc in 1st st, purl to last st, inc in last st.
Work 6 rows in st st without shaping.
Next row: Inc in 1st st, knit to last st, inc.
Work 13 rows without shaping.
Next row: (k2 tog) twice, knit to last 4 sts, (k2 tog) twice. Cast off***.

Front body

Work as Back to **.
Break off main colour and then join in contrast, and work as follows:

Front left bodice

1st row: Inc once in 1st st, k11, turn (slip remaining 8 sts onto a safety pin and leave).
2nd row: p4, knit to end.
3rd row: Inc in 1st st, k12.
4th row: p4, knit to end.
5th row: Inc in 1st st, k13 (15 sts).
Work 7 rows without shaping in garter st, keeping the 4 st st border.
Next row: Cast on 20 sts (for the arm), knit to end of row (35 sts).
Work 13 rows in garter st with the 4 st border as set, without further shaping.
Next row: Cast off 25 sts, k10.
Next row (wrong side facing): Cast off 2 sts, p2, k6 (leave these 8 sts on a spare needle).

Right front bodice

Transfer the first 8 sts left on a safety pin to your knitting needle, with the point of the needle to the middle of the front.
With contrast colour, cast on 4 sts for underlap and then knit across the sts to last st, inc.
Working the 4 st border in st st at centre edge, work right side of bodice to correspond with left side, working all shapings, etc. at opposite ends of needle, until you have 8 sts left.
Slip both fronts onto one needle, making certain that the two borders are in the middle of your work, and with right side of work facing, join in black, and work head from *** to *** as per back.

Head gusset

With black cast on 2 sts.
1st row: Knit.
2nd row: Purl.
3rd row: Inc in both sts.
4th row: Purl.
5th row: Inc, knit to last st, inc.
6th row: Purl.
Repeat the last 2 rows twice.
Work 30 rows in st st.
Next row: Knit, dec at each end of needle.
Next row: Purl.
Repeat the last 2 rows 3 times (2 sts).
Knit one row. Cast off.
With wrong sides of body together, carefully sew up shoulder seams.

Hands

Using black, with right side of work facing you, pick up and knit 15 sts at end of arm.
2nd row: Purl.
3rd row: k6, sl 1, k2 tog, psso, k6.
4th row: Purl.
5th row: k5, sl 1, k2 tog, psso, k5.
6th row: Purl.
7th row: k2 tog, k2, sl 1, k2 tog, psso, k2, k2 tog. Cast off tightly.
Work another hand on the end of the other arm.

Nose

With black cast on 2 sts.
1st row: Inc in both sts.
2nd row and all alternate rows: Purl.
3rd row: Inc, k2, inc.
5th row: Inc, k4, inc.
7th row: Inc, k6, inc.
9th row: Knit.
11th row: k2 tog, k6, k2 tog.
13th row: k2 tog, k4, k2 tog.
15th row: k2 tog, k2, k2 tog.
17th row: k2 tog twice.
Cast off, leaving a length of thread. With a darning needle, use the thread to run a row of gathering sts around the sides of nose and pull in, at the same time adding stuffing gently until the nose is the shape of a round ball. Draw up tightly, and end off.

Left lapel

With contrast, cast on 4 sts.
1st row: Knit.
2nd row: Inc, purl to end.
Repeat the last 2 rows until 12 sts are on needle.
Next row: k2 tog, knit to end.
Next row: Cast off 4 sts, purl to end.
Next row: k2 tog, knit to end.
Next row: Inc in 1st st, purl to end.
Repeat the last 2 rows 3 times. Cast off.

Right lapel

With contrast cast on 4 sts.
1st row: Knit.
2nd row: Purl, inc in last st.

Repeat the last 2 rows until 12 sts are on needle.
Next row: Cast off 4 sts, knit to end.
Next row: p2 tog, purl to end.
Next row: Inc in 1st st, knit to end.
Repeat the last 2 rows 3 times. Cast off.
With main colour work a row of double crochet (US single crochet) around the outside edge of each lapel. If you can't crochet, edge the lapels carefully with bias binding or ribbon, or leave plain.

Coat tails

Using contrast, cast on 2 sts.
1st row: Knit.
2nd row: Inc in 1st st, knit to end.
3rd row: Knit.
Repeat the last 2 rows until there are 15 sts on the needle.
Cast off.
Work another coat tail in the same way.

To make up

Because of the way this Golly is made, the making up is a little different. First overlap the front sections of bodice (when the bodice is facing you the right-hand side should be over the left-hand side) and starting at the top, sew the inside edge of the top border right through to the outside edge of the bottom border. Sew both ends of overlap to give the impression of an opening front. Sew three of the five buttons into position, allowing room at top for the finishing bow.

To sew up head, fold both sides of head piece in half, and mark centre of each with a pin. Fold head gusset in half and mark centre on both sides with a pin. Matching these pins, pin head gusset into position on both sides of head, and sew into position. Finish sewing both sides of head with black, and also the hands. Stuff with filling to shape required (you will find with a gentle squeeze here and there he attains a perfect shape).

With contrast sew up remaining part of shoulder, then finish off the remaining underarm and sides of bodice. Stuff both arms gently but firmly to allow movement at armhole when bodice is stuffed. When stuffing the rest of the bodice, stuff the neck portion tightly, so that head, neck and top of bodice are quite firm—this way the Golly's head stays nice and steady.

Sew up both sides of legs, leaving bottom of feet open. Stuff both legs firmly, especially around the waist section. Finally sew up the bottom of both legs.

Make the eyes out of white and black felt, and glue firmly into place, or you can use plastic sew-on googly eyes. Sew nose into place. Make a happy smiling mouth out of felt and sew or glue into position. Cut a length of faux fur, fold in half and tack along raw edge, and then sew in position on head (from one end of gusset to the other).

Sew straight edge of lapels to the edge of the overlap on both sides of bodice, then sew lapels into position to the neckline, attaching firmly at neck, leaving edged portion free. Finally sew the two coat tails in place at bottom of back bodice, with the straight edges to the centre of the back. Sew a button at each side of join. Finish Golly with a stylish bow tie at the neck.

Ship Ahoy Golly

Illustrated on page 36

This happy 42 cm (16½") tall Golly, in his sleek blue knitted trousers and cheeky blue and white sailor jumper complete with embroidered collar, just asks to be hugged. With his back and front body both knitted in one piece, and with a separate two-piece head, he is quick and easy to knit even for a beginner.

Materials

25 g (1 oz) ball of black 8-ply wool
25 g (1 oz) ball of mid blue 8-ply wool
25 g (1 oz) ball of white 8-ply wool
1 pair 3.25 mm (10) [US 3] knitting needles
length of black faux fur for the hair if you wish, instead of knitting the hair

Tension

7 sts over 2.5 cm (1") width

Back and front (two alike)

Legs

*With black wool or yarn and 3.25 mm (10) [US 3] needles cast on 12 sts and work 10 rows in garter st. Break off black and join in blue.
Next row: Inc in the 1st st, knit to the last st, inc (14 sts).
Next row: Purl.
Work 42 rows in st st*.
Break off blue and leave sts on a safety pin or wool clasp.
Repeat from * to * for other leg.

Body

Knit 14 sts, then knit across the 14 sts from spare needle (28 sts).
Work 8 rows in st st.
Next row: p2 tog, purl to last 2 sts, p2 tog. Break off blue.
Join in white, and continue in garter st as follows:
Work 2 rows of white, 2 rows of blue, until 32 rows have been worked in garter st (16 ribs).

Arms

Continuing in the blue and white stripe pattern as set, cast on 11 sts at beg of next 4 rows.
Work 12 rows on these 70 sts.
Cast off 11 sts at beg of next 4 rows.
Cast off 5 sts at beg next 2 rows. Cast off remaining sts.

Hands

Join shoulder and top arm seams (leaving the last cast-off sts of back and front unsewn).
With right side of work facing and using black, pick up and knit 14 sts evenly along end of arm.
Work 7 rows in garter st, and then cast off 2 sts at beg of next 2 rows.
Work 3 rows straight in garter st. Cast off.
Work hand on end of other sleeve to match.

Head (back and front alike)

With black cast on 14 sts and work in st st as follows:
Inc 1 st at each end of 4th and every following 3rd row until there are 24 sts on your needle. (Tie a coloured thread to last st at each end of the needle—this is where you will start the hair from.)
Work 8 rows in st st without increasing.
Dec 1 st at each end of next and every following 3rd row until 14 sts remain.
Work 1 row straight. Cast off.

Hair

(This step is optional, especially for the beginner knitter—use black faux fur sewn across the top of the head if you prefer.)

With right side of head facing you, rejoin black wool at right edge where you tied coloured thread, pick up and knit 42 sts evenly to other side of head.

Next row: *Insert the needle into next st, wind wool round the needle and forefinger of left hand (as if you were to knit) twice, draw the three loops through, then slip the loops back onto the left hand needle, and then knit all loops tog, repeat from * to end. Cast off.

Repeat on other head piece.

Sailor collar

Using blue wool cast on 28 sts and work 2 rows in garter st.

1st row: Knit.

2nd row: k2, purl to last 2 sts, k2.

Repeat the last 2 rows 7 times.

Next row: k9, cast off 10 sts, knit to end.

Continue on the last 9 sts as follows:

1st row: k1, k2 tog, purl to end of row

2nd row: Knit.

3rd row: k2, purl to end of row.

4th row: Knit.

*Repeat the last four rows until 2 sts remain.

Work 30 rows straight on these 2 sts (tie). Cast off*.

Join in wool to other side.

1st row: Purl to the last 3 sts, k2 tog, k1.

2nd row: Knit.

3rd row: Purl to last 2 sts, k2.

4th row: Knit.

Work from * to * for other side of collar.

To make up

Join back and front bodies together along sides. Fold legs so that the side seams meet at the centre, sew up inside leg seams, then join the foot seam. Stuff firmly.

Join both head sections together, leaving the neck open, making sure you don't catch in the loops of the hair. Stuff to the required firmness, but don't stuff out of shape. Attach head firmly to the body using ladder stitch, adding extra stuffing if needed.

With white wool, work a row of chain stitch just inside the garter st border of the sailor collar to give that added nautical effect. Place the sailor collar around neck and tie in a knot at the front.

Cut out the eye shapes required in black and white felt, and the mouth in red felt, pin in place, then attach using clear-drying craft glue.

Drummin' Golly

Illustrated on page 36

Quick and simple to knit, this 41 cm (16") Golly traces his origins to the very early years of World War II. He can be made in just a few hours, and is therefore ideal for that last minute gift for a child, or for a fete. The body consists of just two pieces (with even the coat tails included in the back body) with head, hands and collar added afterwards.

Materials

25 g (1 oz) of 8-ply wool in red or other colour for trousers
25 g (1 oz) of 8-ply in blue or other colour for jacket
25 g (1 oz) of 8-ply in black for head and feet
small amount of 8-ply in white for hands
length of black faux fur (if you don't wish to try 'knotting' the hair yourself)
1 pair of 3.25 mm (10) [US 3] knitting needles
2 spare needles
2 sew-on plastic googly eyes
small piece of red felt or velvet for mouth
5 or 6 buttons for decoration
crochet hook

Tension

6 sts over 2.5 cm (1") width

1st coat tail

With 3.25 mm (10) [US 3] needles and colour chosen for jacket, cast on 2 sts.
1st row: Knit.
2nd row: Inc in the 1st st, knit to end.
Repeat these 2 rows until there are 10 sts on the needle. Break off wool.
Leave these stitches on a spare needle.

2nd coat tail

Cast on 2 sts.
1st row: Knit.
2nd row: k1, inc in next st.
3rd row: Knit.
4th row: k1, inc in next st, k1.
5th row: Knit.
6th row: Knit to 2nd last st, inc, k1.
Repeat rows 5 and 6 until there are 10 sts on the needle.
Slip these 10 sts onto the spare needle with the first 10 sts, with the two straight edges in the middle.

Back

Worked from the feet up. With black wool, cast on 10 sts and knit 10 rows.
Change to the colour you have chosen for the trousers and work 40 rows in st st. Leave this leg on a spare needle. Make a second leg to match.
Next row: Knit the second leg and also the first leg onto one needle (20 sts).
Work 21 rows in st st on these 20 sts, starting with a purl row.
Next row: Place the 20 coat tail sts in front of the 20 body sts. With your jacket colour wool, knit a coat st together with the corresponding body st as 1 st, repeat along the row to the end (20 sts).
Knit 21 rows in garter st.
Cast on 22 sts at beginning of the next 2 rows.
Knit 12 rows.
Cast off 10 sts at beginning of each next 4 rows. Cast off the remaining sts.

Front

Work exactly the same as the back, but omitting the coat tails.

Head

With black wool, cast on 10 sts.
1st row: Knit.
2nd row: Purl.
3rd row: Knit.
4th row: Inc in the 1st st, purl to the last st, inc.
Repeat these 4 rows 3 times.
Work 10 rows in st st.

Next row: Work 2 sts tog at both ends of row.
Repeat the last row until 10 sts remain. Cast off.
Work another piece the same for the other side of head.
Sew the back body to the front body, along the shoulder seams only, leaving neck portion open.

Hands (gloves)

With right side of work facing, and using white wool, pick up and knit 14 sts evenly along end of sleeve.
Work 10 rows in st st.
Next row: k2 tog, knit to last 2 sts, k2 tog.
Next row: Purl. Cast off.
Work another hand to match.

Collar

With white wool, cast on 24 sts.
1st row: Knit.
2nd row: Knit, inc 1 st at beginning and end of row.
Repeat the last 2 rows 3 times. Cast off.

To make up

Join the back body piece to the front body piece, sewing up all side seams, but leaving the neck open.

Stuff the body firmly. Join the sides of the head, leaving neck open. Stuff head firmly, but still keeping the rather flattish shape of a Golly head. Sew the head to the body.

Sew on eyes. Use clear-drying craft glue to attach mouth.

Hair

Wind black wool around a strip of cardboard (or a wooden or metal ruler) 2.5 cm (1") wide.

Cut the wool along one edge. Double each 5 cm (2") length of wool, draw the loop through a stitch in the head (using a crochet hook) and pull the ends tightly through the loop.

Work this type of hair 'fringe' along seam line, from where the ear would be if the Golly had ears, across head to the other ear. Sew the collar around neck, and finish with a bow of your choice at the front. Stitch two buttons at the back just above the coat tails, and 3 or 4 buttons down the front of the jacket.

Sewn Gollies

Wally Golly

Illustrated on page 37

This little 26 cm (10¼") Golly is based on one that I learnt to make sitting at the kitchen table of my childhood home in Geelong, Victoria, with black-out blinds at the windows, during World War II. Made entirely in felt, even his hair, using patterns that were printed on brown paper, and sold for 1 shilling (10 cents), this Golly was made under the guidance of Red Cross volunteers by many repatriated servicemen convalescing after war injuries.

When you make this Golly I hope you, too, enjoy recreating a little of our past history in toy making.

I have altered the original pattern just a little by shortening his very long legs, altering his original bow and making his hands a little larger, but at the same time keeping his lovely fat tummy and sway back. Although originally designed to be sewn by hand (turnings allowed for) as I have made him, he could also be sewn by machine, but a small seam allowance would have to be added to the pattern.

Materials

2 squares of felt in colour chosen for trousers
1 square of felt in colour chosen for jacket
2 squares of black felt for head, feet, hands, hair and eyes
small piece of white felt for collar and eyes
scrap of contrast felt for bow back
scrap of red felt for mouth

To make up

Following the pattern, cut out all the pieces required in the colours you have chosen.

1. Sew the centre front seam of the two front jacket halves B–C, and then sew the centre back seam of the two jacket backs E–F.
2. Sew the two pieces of the front trousers together along centre front C–X, and then sew two back trousers together along centre back F–X.
3. Sew front of jacket D–D to top of front trousers D–D. Ensure you work all oversewn seams on same side of work.
4. Sew back jacket G–G to top of back trousers G–G.
5. Sew up front and back seams of each foot, then sew soles of feet into place matching XX with XX and OO with OO. Leaving top of foot open, stuff firmly.
6. Sew around both hands from wrist to wrist, leaving wrists open. Stuff firmly, stuffing thumb section first.
7. Starting at the neck A, sew across shoulders to wrist on both sides. Then sew from bottom of wrists, along sleeve seams, down side seams of jacket and down side seams of trousers. Leaving bottom of leg open, sew up inside leg seams, working several small stitches at X, so as to make this joint firm.
8. Place hand inside wrist, with thumbs facing inwards, matching outside seam, and sew hand in place. Overstitch the little part of sleeve left unsewn. Repeat for other hand.
9. With toe of foot facing towards the front, place the middle of the side of foot to side seam and pin in place, position inside seam to middle of the other side of foot and pin in place. Sew foot to bottom of leg, catching across instep and at heel. Oversew any of trouser leg unsewn to form flares. Repeat for other leg.
10. Stuff body, starting from the legs; stuff to waist, then stuff each arm, before stuffing from waist up to neck.
11. Sew around head, leaving neck open. Stuff head firmly. Sew head to body adding any extra stuffing you may feel necessary to give a good stiff neck.
12. Sew the two front sections of collar to back collar, matching M and N. Place collar around neck and join at front with a couple of stitches.

13. Cut out larger bow in contrast, and smaller bow in same colour as jacket. Place smaller collar on top of larger collar and run a series of gathering stitches across the centre, draw up, and then sew a short length of contrast around centre of bow, stitching at the back. Sew the completed bow into position at base of neck.

14. Cut out fringe from black felt, fold in half, pin along fold to keep everything even, and then carefully cut down towards pins at even distances all along piece.

15. Ease the fringe around the head seam, pin in position, then sew fringe in place at the front of the head, and then sew again at the back Hey Presto—Wally Golly!

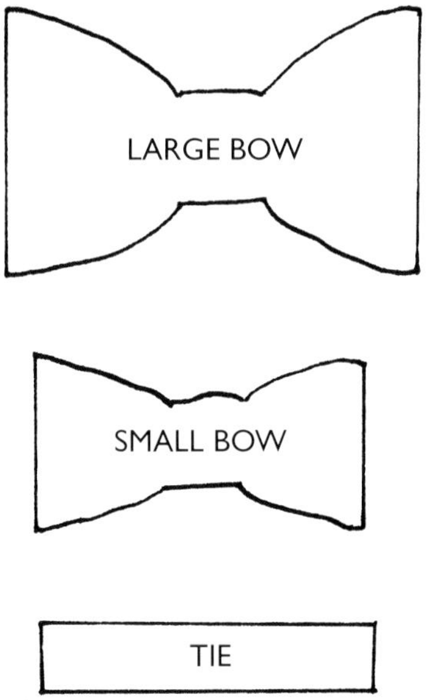

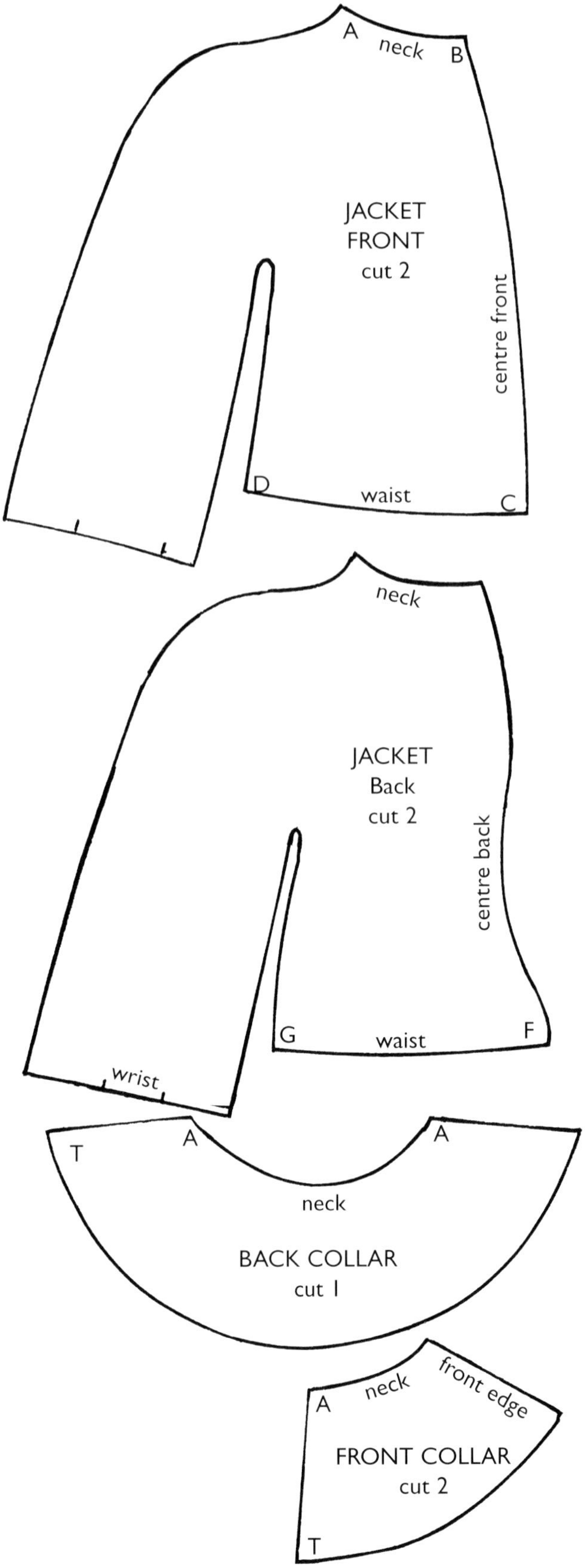

Wally Golly pattern layout

Actual Size

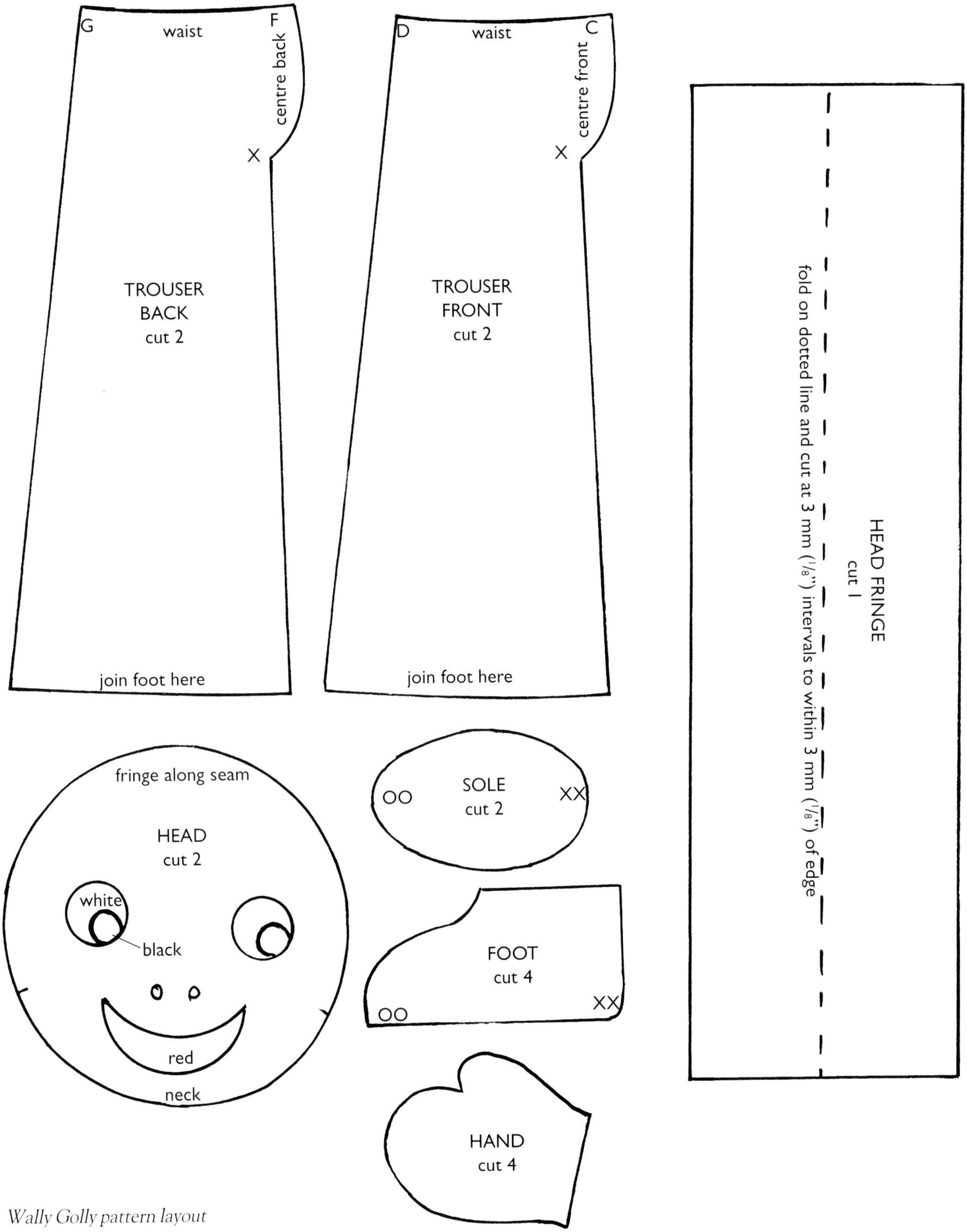

Wally Golly pattern layout

Actual Size

Hi-Jinks Golly

Illustrated on page 37

The unusual methods employed in giving this 36 cm (14") Golly his shape and movement, such as being able to bend at the knees and hips through the use of backstitch, are hidden when he is dressed in his smart tailcoat, vest and trousers. The Golly's body is quite quick and simple to make as his head, arms and torso are made from just two pieces, with strong gathering threads to give him his head and hand shapings. Once Golly is dressed in his smart attire he can give wonderful high-kicking performances, while at the same time sitting 'demurely' in a chair!

Materials

30 cm (12") of black felt or other material
30 cm (12") of material or felt for trousers
30 cm (12") of contrast felt or fabric for his tail coat
1 square of white or contrasting felt or fabric for vest
small scrap of red felt for mouth
pair of googly plastic eyes (or use black and white felt)
length of ribbon for bow tie
4 gold buttons

Seam allowance If you are making the Golly's body in felt, follow the seam allowances given in the pattern pieces. If you are using fabric for the body, allow an extra 5 mm ($^3/_{16}$") for seams when cutting out. Seam allowances are included on all clothing pattern pieces.

Method

Cut out all the pieces required—two pieces of torso, which are cut on the fold, four leg pieces, four foot pieces, and two soles.

Feet

Begin by making up both feet, with the right sides of material together and matching notches. Leave open at the top and bottom. Place sole of foot with the OO and XX matching on each foot. Turn each foot right side out and stuff.

Legs

Sew up each leg matching notches and leaving open at top (A–B) and at bottom (CC–DD). Run a gathering thread around the bottom of each leg.

With right sides together, pin the front seam of the foot NN to the front seam of leg at DD. Pin back seam of foot MM to back seam of leg at CC. Gently pull gathering thread until leg fits evenly around foot. Sew foot to leg. Repeat for other leg. Turn legs right side out.

Stuff each leg gently but firmly to where indicated by the broken line. With front seam B–DD facing you, gently squeeze the leg until back seam and front seam are aligned, then stitch right across the leg using a backstitch, ending off securely at each side. This allows the leg to bend at the knee, enabling Golly to sit in a chair. Stuff rest of leg. Repeat with other leg.

Torso

Sew right around torso, leaving open from AA to AA at top of head for later stuffing, also leaving open at bottom of torso where legs will be joined. Turn right side out. If using fabric instead of felt, make a small hem at bottom of torso.

Hands

Stuff each hand section, then run a strong gathering thread around each wrist where designated, and pull up to form wrist, ending off securely.

Attaching the legs

Holding the tops of the two legs even, with feet to front, run a tacking stitch across both legs (make sure the feet are facing in the same direction). Place legs inside the body between B–B, with the two legs meeting at A. Tack in position, then using a ladder stitch or small backstitch, sew both legs firmly into position. This allows your Golly to bend at the thighs.

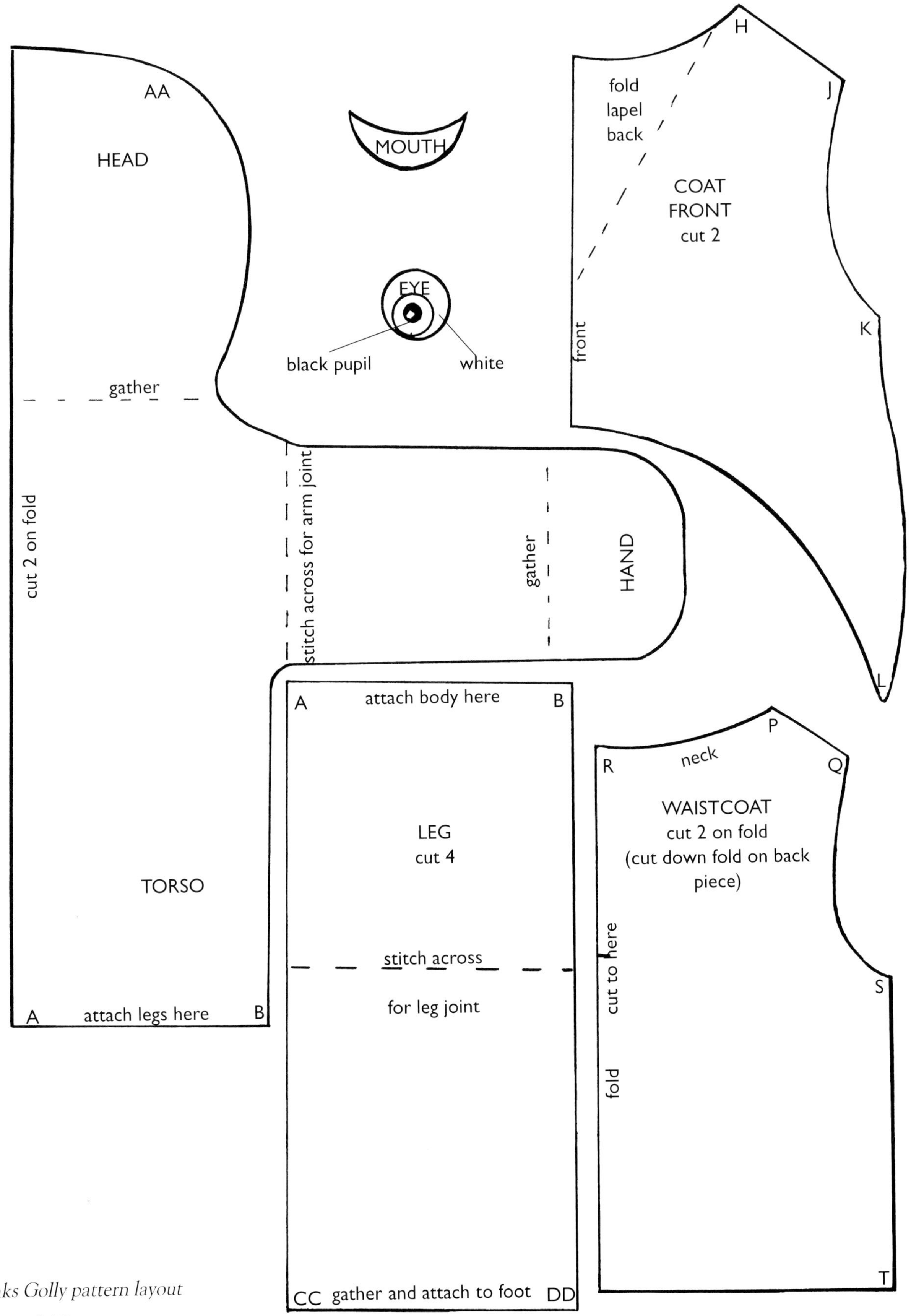

Hi-jinks Golly pattern layout

Enlarge 125%

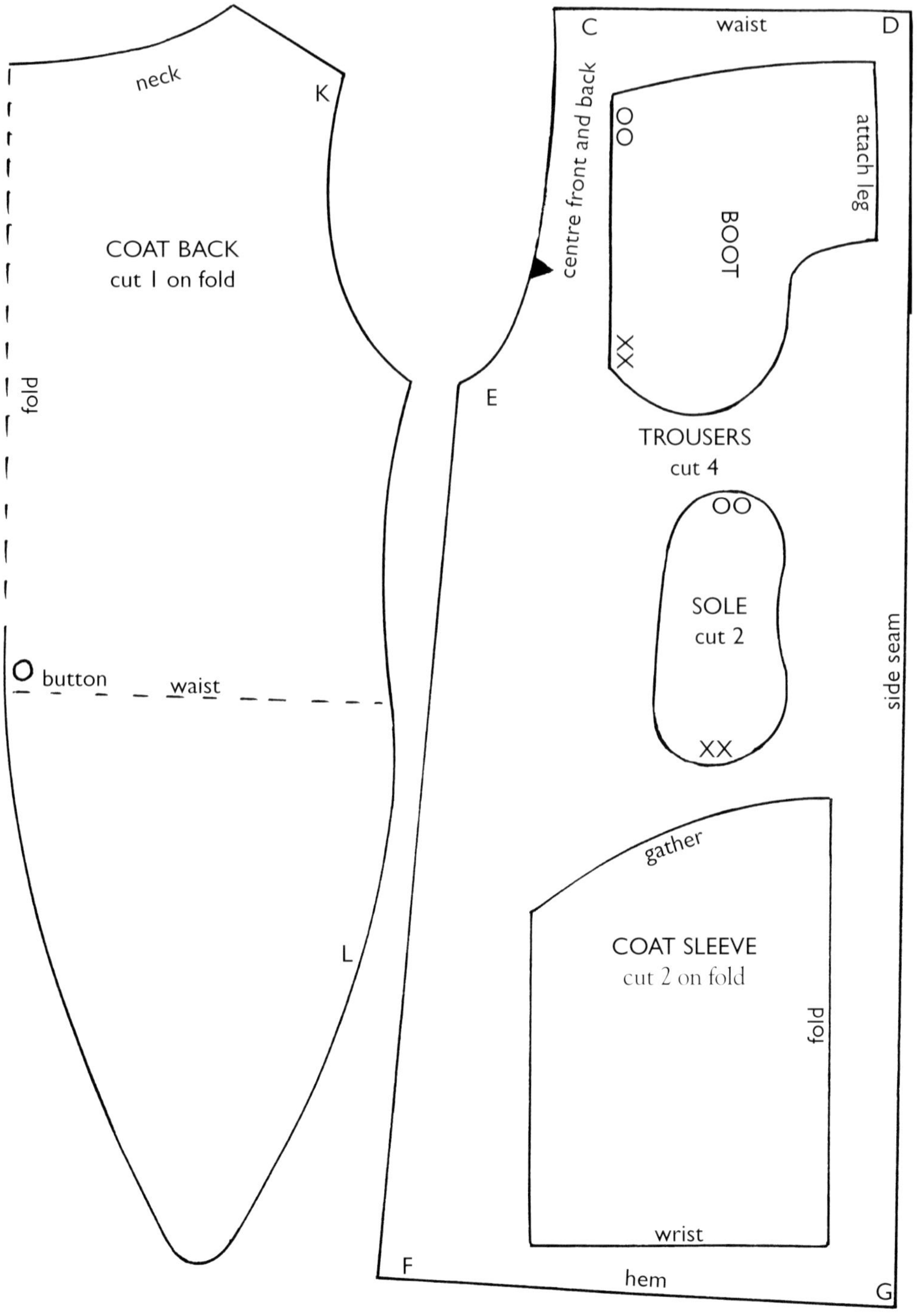

Hi-jinks Golly pattern layout

Enlarge 125%

Stuffing the torso

Stuff Golly torso quite firmly, first stuffing the arms (leaving a small gap at the 'armhole' to allow some movemement in this area), then stuffing the rest of the torso until you reach the neck area.

Head

Thread a needle with strong cotton and then make a line of gathering stitches where indicated at the neck; pull in quite firmly to form neck and end off securely.

Stuff the head firmly to shape, and then finish off the gap between AA–AA with ladder stitch, or oversew.

Fold a 5 cm (2") strip of black faux fur in half, and sew the raw edges together. Sew hair in position on Golly, using ladder stitch, attaching first at the front of the head, and then at the back.

Stitch or glue on Golly's eyes and mouth as shown.

Trousers

Sew centre front and centre back of trousers, matching notches. With right sides of trousers together, and matching notches, sew down side seams and inside leg seams. Leaving wrong side out, try trousers on Golly. Turn over a 1 cm ($^{3}/_{8}$") facing at waist, pin; turn up the hem to fit and pin. Take off trousers, hem the bottom of each leg, and then either make two darts in the front of trousers or gather to fit waist. Place finished trousers on Golly.

Vest

Cut out the two pieces of vest, cutting one piece down the fold seam to point indicated for back of vest. Sew up shoulder seams from P to Q. Make a small hem around neckline and also around each armhole. Sew up side seams, and then hem bottom of vest. Try on Golly, and using a hook and eye or press stud, join at back of neck.

Coat

I used felt for the coat, but if you are using fabric you will have to face the front edge so that you can turn back the top of each jacket front to act as lapels.

Cut out the five coat pieces—2 fronts, one back (cut on fold) and two sleeves. Sew shoulder seams H–J. Place sleeves in armholes with matching notches, ease if necessary and sew into position. Join side seams from K–L. You will notice that the side seam doesn't go all the way; this gives the coat its tail-coat effect.

Place coat on Golly, turn back the top edge of jacket to act as lapels, sew buttons down the front, and one button at each side of split at back.

Finish off at neck with a nice bright bow tie.

LEFT: OZZIE GOLLY, resplendent in his green and gold 8-ply outfit, wonders whether his 36 cm (14") length could possibly fit behind the dashboard of the old wooden truck. Note the round nose frequently seen in old-style Gollies. What a wonderful mascot he would make (page 20)

LEFT: DRUMMIN' GOLLY is set to wake up all those sleepyheads. This design dating back to the early 1940s can be knitted in 8-ply in no time at all (page 25)

RIGHT: SHIP AHOY GOLLY, 42 cm (16½") tall and dressed in a brand new 8-ply outfit, dreams of maybe one day being the captain of a boat just like the Australian-made plastic boat sitting on the table beside him (page 23)

RIGHT: WALLY GOLLY, based on a 1940s wartime paper pattern, draws himself up to his full 26 cm (10¼") height beside a 1917 children's annual which features a Golly on the cover (page 28)

LEFT: HI-JINKS GOLLY Sitting on an old wooden toy piano, Hi-Jinks Golly, 36 cm (14") tall, is seeing if he can still touch his toes. The special jointing at knees and hips allows him to sit in adventurous positions (page 31)

Right: JOLLY GOLLIES The larger 38 cm (15") Golly, adapted from an early 1940s pattern, keeps a careful brotherly eye on Junior, the half-size 19 cm (7½") version of the same pattern (page 39).
Bottom Right: Detail shows the triangular nose of the smaller Jolly Golly (page 39)

Jolly Gollies

Illustrated on page 38

These two loveable Gollies date from the early years of World War II; at this time commercially made toys were practically impossible to buy, as many firms had been shut down completely. Other firms resorted to printing patterns from which toys could be made at home. Jolly Golly has been adapted from a pattern printed by Joy Toys during this time. (Joy Toys was once a well known Australian toy firm manufacturing teddy bears and other soft toys.)

The larger of the two Gollies is 38 cm (15") high—the original size. As reproducing this pattern full size would take up too much space and exclude other patterns, it has been reduced to half size, hence the 19 cm (7½") Golly with his lovely little added triangular nose.

You can, of course, make this lovely Golly to any size you wish via the medium of the photocopy machine. To bring the pattern up to its original size increase by 200 per cent; if you want it smaller or even larger again, use your own choice of reduction or enlargement.

A word of warning: When reducing or enlarging a pattern by photocopying, always check the resulting pattern of the clothes before making up to ensure the fit is correct.

Materials

38 cm (15") Golly:

30 cm (12") of velvet, felt or other black fabric
5 cm (2") strip of black faux fur
small piece of black felt for eyes
small piece of white felt for eyes or pair of plastic googly eyes
small piece of red felt for mouth

Clothes

25 cm (10") of striped or check fabric for trousers—I used striped velvet
2 squares of felt for jacket in colour desired
1 square of white felt or 25 cm (10") square of fabric for shirt
1 gold button

19 cm (7½") Golly:

2 squares of black felt
4 cm (1°") strip black faux fur for hair
small piece of white felt for eyes
small piece of red felt for mouth

Clothes

small piece of check or striped material for trousers
1 square of felt in colour of your choice for jacket
small scrap of white fabric or felt for the shirt (fabric is best for this size)
length of ribbon for bow
1 small button or gold bead for final touch

Note: Where 5 mm (3/16") seams are allowed on 38 cm (15") Golly, on a smaller Golly made of felt a smaller seam is needed. This is achieved by oversewing.

Body

1. Matching notches, sew the front feet on the ends of the legs of the front body.
2. Likewise join the back feet matching notches, and sew the dart seams where shown.
3. Sew back and front bodies together at shoulders, matching notches where shown.
4. Stitch together arms at thumbs side only, matching notches. Sew each arm to matching notches at back and front of body pieces, making sure the thumb side is facing upwards.
5. Pin both sides of Golly's body together, making sure that the underarm seams meet, and the feet meet at the notches.
6. Commencing at one arm, where you left off sewing, sew around Golly's body, sewing down one side of body, around the legs and feet, up the other side, and finishing where you left off on the other arm—leaving the neck opening free.

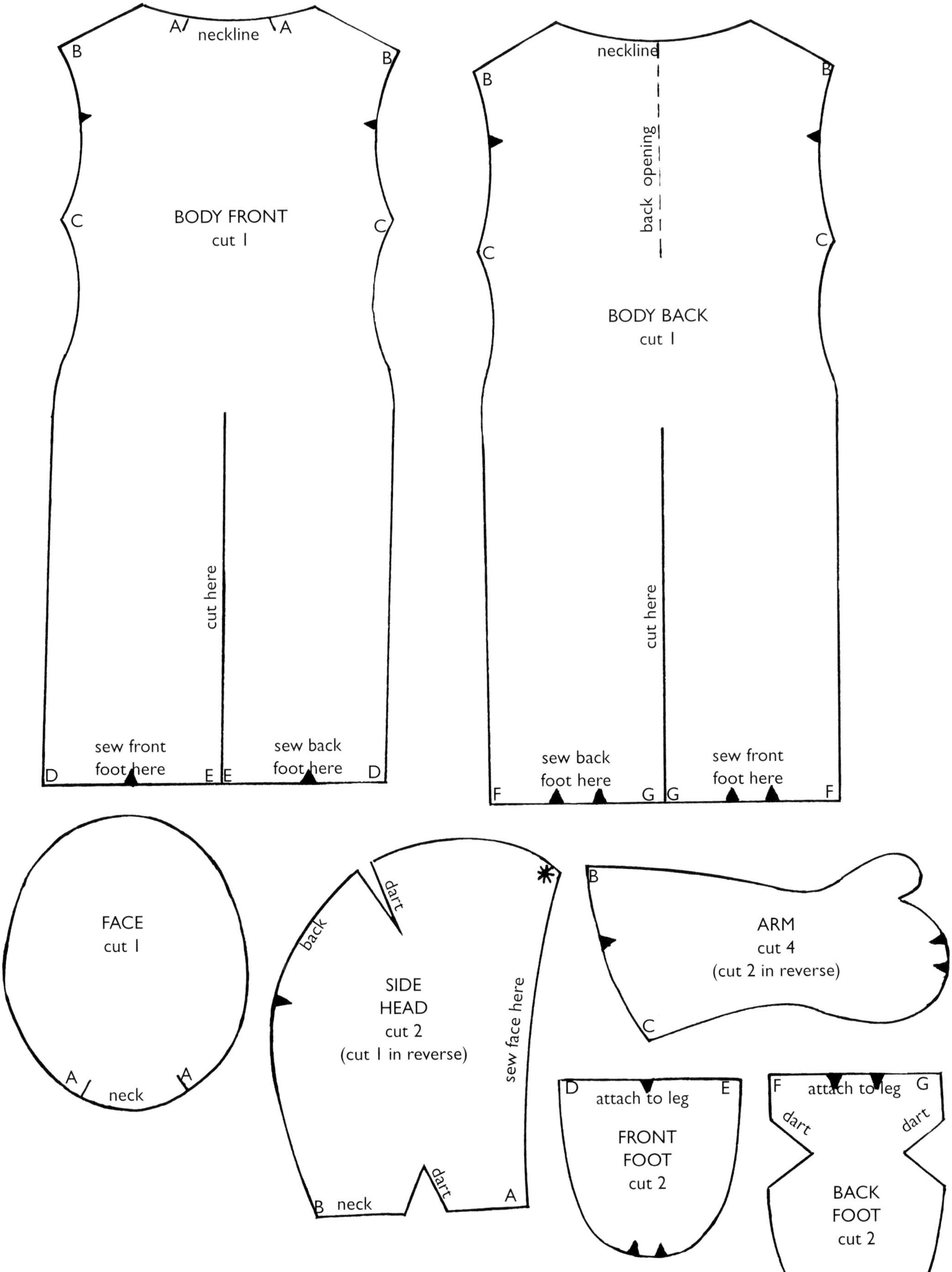

Jolly Golly pattern layout

Actual Size

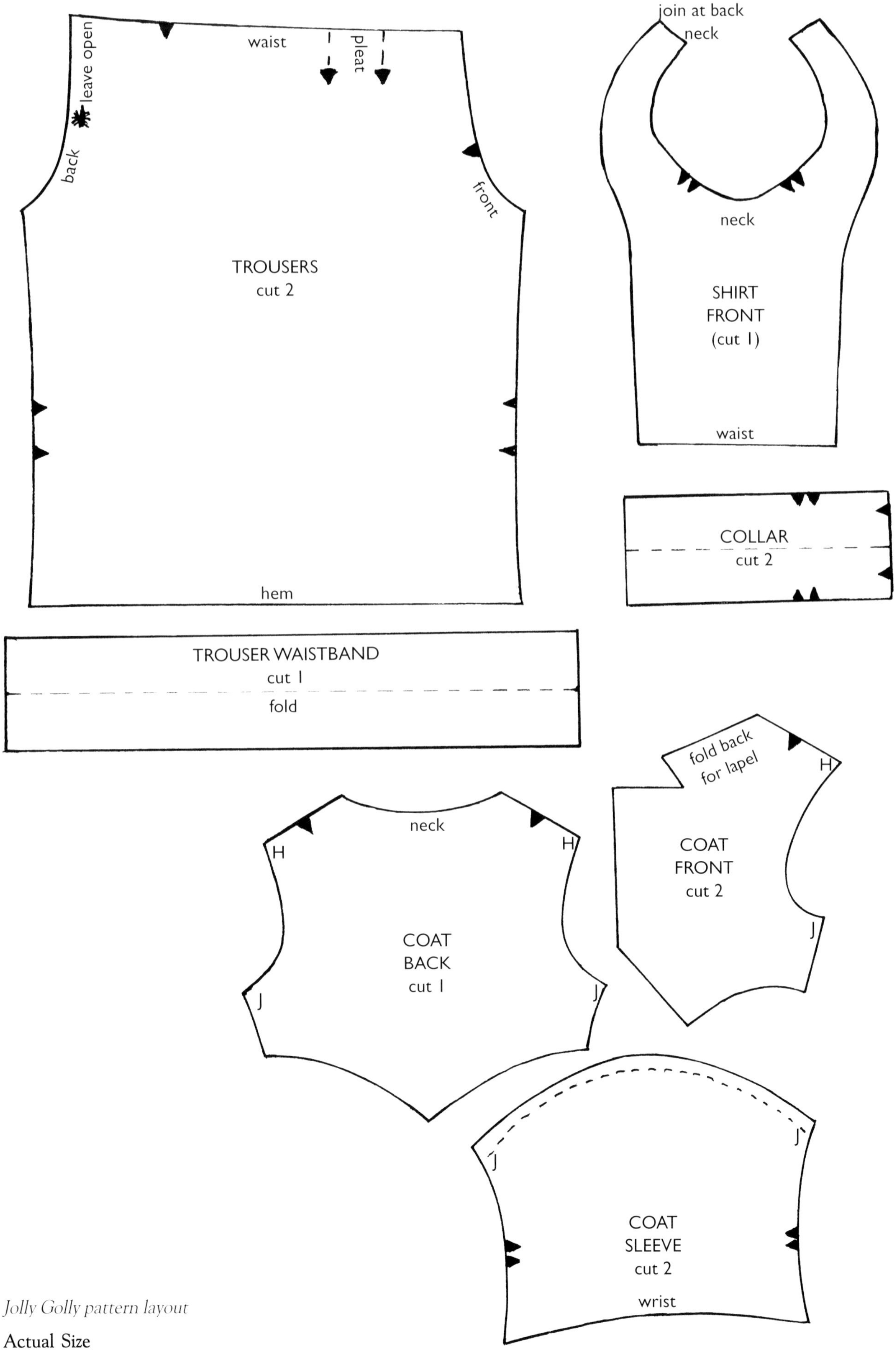

Jolly Golly pattern layout

Actual Size

7. Turn body right side out.
8. Stuff each leg to the top, and then if you wish machine or backstitch across top of both legs. This acts as a hinge so the legs can swing freely.
9. If you wish the arms to also move freely at the armhole, stuff to armhole, and then sew across from the shoulder to the underarm.
10. Stuff rest of body up to neck.

Head

1. Sew the darts on both side head pieces, then with right sides of material facing, sew the two pieces together along the longer curve.
2. Fold face in half lengthwise, and mark the centre top and bottom of the face. With right side of material facing, match the centre of the face to the top seam of head, ease face piece around both sides of head back.
   Note: The bottom part of the face piece remains unsewn. Turn right side out.
3. Stuff the head firmly.
4. Mark the centre front of body, and the bottom centre front of face, and pin in position. Gently ease body and head portions to match, pinning as you go.
5. Sew the head firmly to the body, at the same time adding any stuffing necessary to make the torso/neck/head section area nice and firm.
6. Fold the strip of faux fur in half, and stitch along cut edge. Pin hair in place around head as shown in photograph. Sew the hair firmly in place, first sewing the fur to the face from the front, and then from the back.
7. Cut out the eye pieces. Glue the black pupils in place on the white pieces and then glue finished eyes in place on head with clear-drying craft glue.
8. Cut out mouth and glue in place.

Trousers

1. Sew the centre front seams matching notches. Sew the centre back seams together to where marked, leaving top part of seam open.
2. Stitch the inside leg seams, matching notches.
3. Make a small pleat on each side of the front seam at the position marked.
4. With the right sides of trousers and waistband together, pin in place, matching the notches. Sew the waistband to the trousers, then fold the band over and hem the inner edge into position. Finish off with either a hook and eye or a snap fastener.

Shirt

1. Fold collar lengthwise and stitch notched ends together. Turn right side out.
2. Stitch the two halves of the collar to the neck of the shirt, matching notches. If using fabric make small hems at sides and bottom of shirt—this step is not necessary if using felt, as it would make the shirt too bulky.
3. Fasten shirt together at the back of the neck with small hook and eye.

Coat

1. Sew the shoulder seams of the coat, matching notches.
2. Ease the sleeve to fit into the armhole and sew in place.
3. Stitch the sleeve seam and side seam of the coat, matching the notches.
4. Turn back the lapels of the coat and fasten at front with a gold button.
5. Make a bow tie out of either ribbon or matching trouser fabric. Fold a length of ribbon or fabric in half, with join at the middle of back section. Gather across middle, and then sew a narrower piece over gathering, ending off at back of bow. Sew finished bow in place at front of shirt collar.

Golly Dude

Illustrated on page 48

A 32 cm (12½") Golly whose clothes are an integral part of his body. He is quite quick to make and can be made all in felt or a combination of fabrics and felt.

Materials

1 square of black felt for face, hands, feet and eyes
1 square of black faux fur for hair
small piece of check fabric for trousers
1 square of contrast felt for jacket (torso)
small piece of felt for waistcoat
small piece of contrast felt for lapels
3 dark buttons
small piece of red felt for mouth
small piece of white felt for eyes
checked ribbon for bow tie

To make up

1. Cut out 2 trouser pieces on the fold.
2. Cut out front and back torso (both on the fold).
3. Sew back coat tails to top of right side of the back pants.
4. With the right sides together sew back torso to back pants, with coat tails sandwiched between, then sew front torso to front pants.
5. With right sides together, sew from neck to wrist on torso, then from wrist to ankle. Repeat on the other side of Golly. Sew up inside leg seam. Turn right side out.
6. Sew around shoes, leaving open from W to X. Turn right side out. Stuff firmly.
7. Turn under a small hem on trousers and pin trousers to shoes with centre front X matching centre front shoe X. Sew trouser leg to shoe, easing in as necessary to fit shoe.
8. Stuff to waist, stuffing each trouser leg quite firmly.
9. Sew around each hand from F to G, leaving wrist section open. Turn right side out and stuff firmly.
10. With thumbs facing inwards to body, sew the bottom of the torso sleeve over each hand.
11. Stuff arms firmly, and then stuff rest of torso.
12. Cut face out of felt and back of head out of faux black fur.
13. With right sides together, carefully pin faux fur to face, stroking hair inwards as you go. Sew around head, leaving space open at bottom for stuffing. Turn right side out.
14. Sew head to body, adding any extra stuffing necessary to strengthen neck area.
15. With right sides facing, sew the two side lapels to front of the waistcoat. Press seam with fingers so that lapels lie nearly flat with jacket. Sew lapels and waistcoat carefully onto jacket, down lapel seam, keeping the centre of the waistcoat in line with centre of torso and head. If you wish you can sew the top of the lapels to the shoulder seam. Sew three decorative buttons down front.
16. Glue black pupil to the white eye felt, and then glue eye into position with clear-drying craft glue. Glue mouth in position. Finish off with a checked bow.

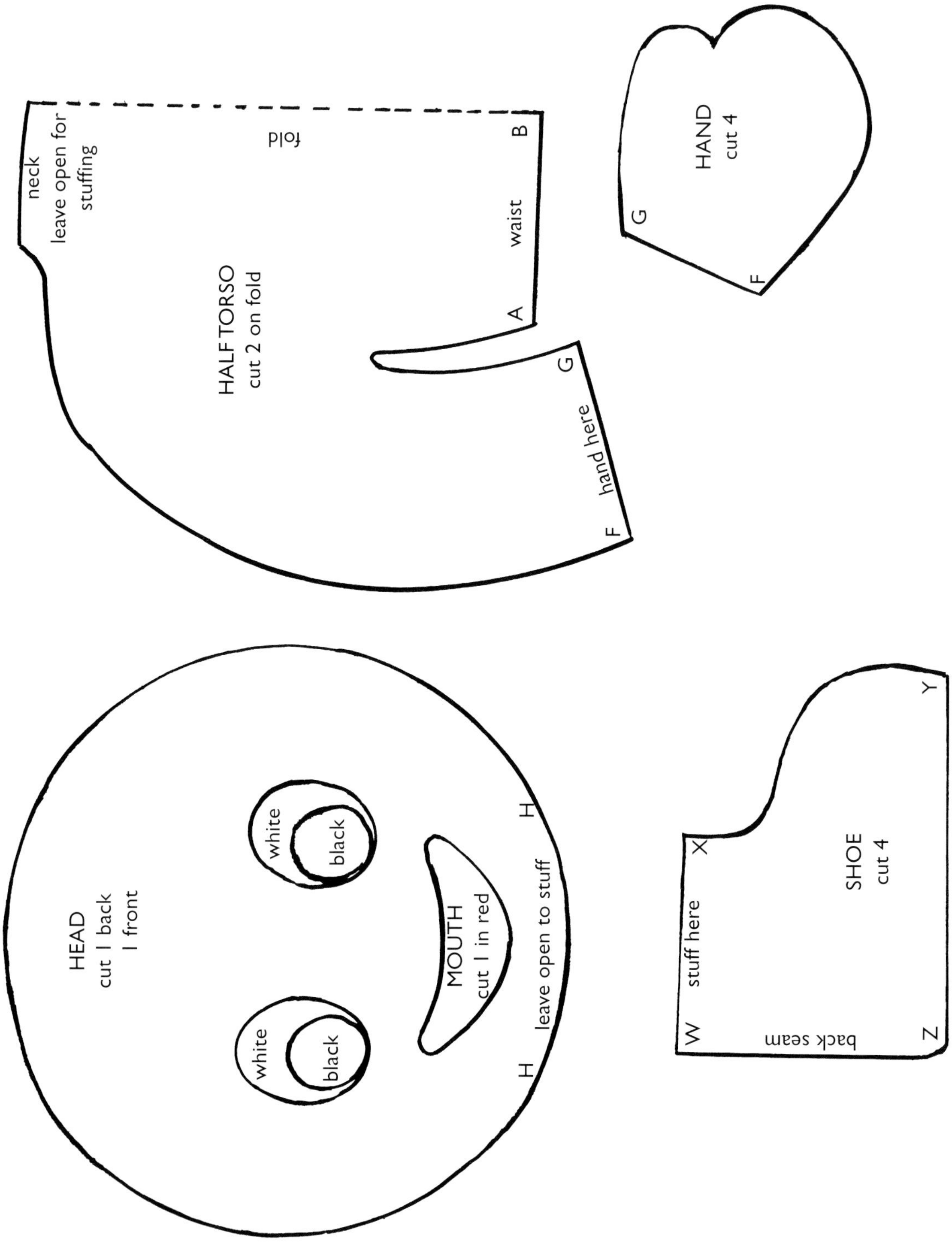

Golly Dude pattern layout

Actual size

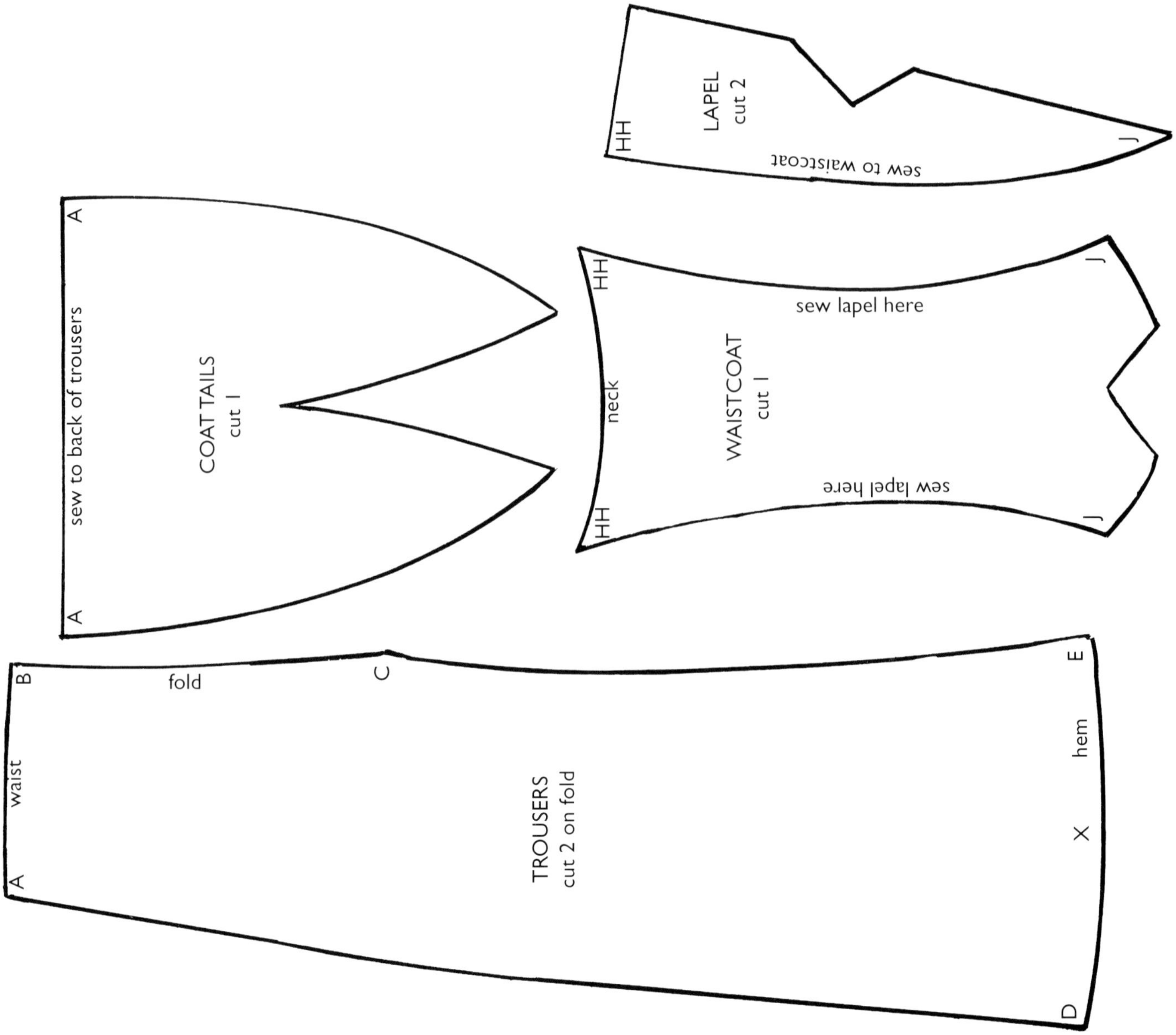

Golly Dude pattern layout

Actual size

Golly Dazzler

Illustrated on page 47

Made entirely in felt, this 20 cm (8") Golly at first glance looks quite simple, but he does take a little more skill and care to make, especially his body with its shaped legs and arms and nicely shaped one-piece head and torso. His clothes are quite easy but have a finely tailored look when finished. With judicious choice of colour, or with turn-back cuffs and bottom jacket lapels decorated with glitter, this Golly will quickly live up to the name Dazzler.

Materials

1 square of black felt
1 square of green felt or colour of your choice for trousers
1 square of wine felt or colour of your choice for jacket
1 square of yellow felt or colour of your choice for vest
small scrap of white felt for collar
small scrap of red felt for mouth
small piece of black faux fur for hair
2 white sequins for eyes
2 black beads for pupils
gold beads for buttons
glitter for decoration (optional)
Note: To get the best and most tailored look on this Golly use small oversew stitches throughout.

Body

Cut out the 4 leg pieces, 2 foot soles, 4 arm pieces and 2 torso pieces as per pattern.

Legs

Sew both legs by matching notches, leaving open at top and bottom of leg. Sew base of foot, matching OO and XX to the bottom of leg. Carefully turn each leg right side out and stuff.

Arms

Sew around the two arm pieces, being extra careful around the thumb area, and leaving open at armhole end. Repeat with other arm. Turn right side out and stuff carefully, gently but firmly stuffing the thumb section first.

Torso

Sew around torso leaving open at the top of head for stuffing. With centre front seam of legs facing the front, tack legs in position at base of torso. Sew firmly in place.
Stuff rest of body firmly, making sure that the Golly has nice shoulders, and then ladder stitch or oversew the opening at the top of the head.
Pin the stuffed arms in position where shown on pattern, and then using ladder stitch carefully sew each arm in place. Golly is now ready to dress.

Trousers

Cut out the two trouser pieces and join side seams and inside leg seams, matching notches. Try on Golly to see if any alteration to length is needed. Turn right side out, sew a line of gathering stitches around waist, place trousers on Golly, pull in gathers to fit waist and tie off securely.

Vest

Join shoulder seams and side seams. Place on Golly and either glue in place, or using tiny stitches sew up down the front, placing left side of vest over right side (see photograph).

Jacket

Sew up shoulder seams, then fit and sew sleeves to jacket, easing a little at shoulder if necessary. Sew up sleeve seams and side seams of jacket. Place on Golly, and then turn back bottom of sleeves to form cuff. Catch top of jacket at neck, and turn back at bottom edge of front to give the lapel effect.

Above: GOLLY DAZZLER 'Will I make the party on time?' wonders this 20 cm (8") tall Golly as checks the time on a one-twelfth scale grandfather clock that really works (page 46)

ABOVE: GOLLY DUDE, 32 cm (12½") tall, is busy telling Ted all about the party he is going to tonight (page 43)

RIGHT: 'Watch the birdie' says GOLLY GOSH, just 13.5 cm (5¼") tall and crocheted in 4-ply, as he stands beside the lovely one-twelfth scale model of an old professional photographer's camera, made by my husband Jim (page 54)

BELOW: WOOLLY GOLLIES 'I told you not to touch that button!' says one 10 cm (4") Woolly Golly to the other as the old 'Cat' jack-in-the-box pops its head up and frightens them both (page 62)

LEFT: D.C. GOLLY 'Hold on tight and off we'll go', says D.C. Golly as he takes young Golly Gosh for a ride on a Mamod steam engine (page 56)

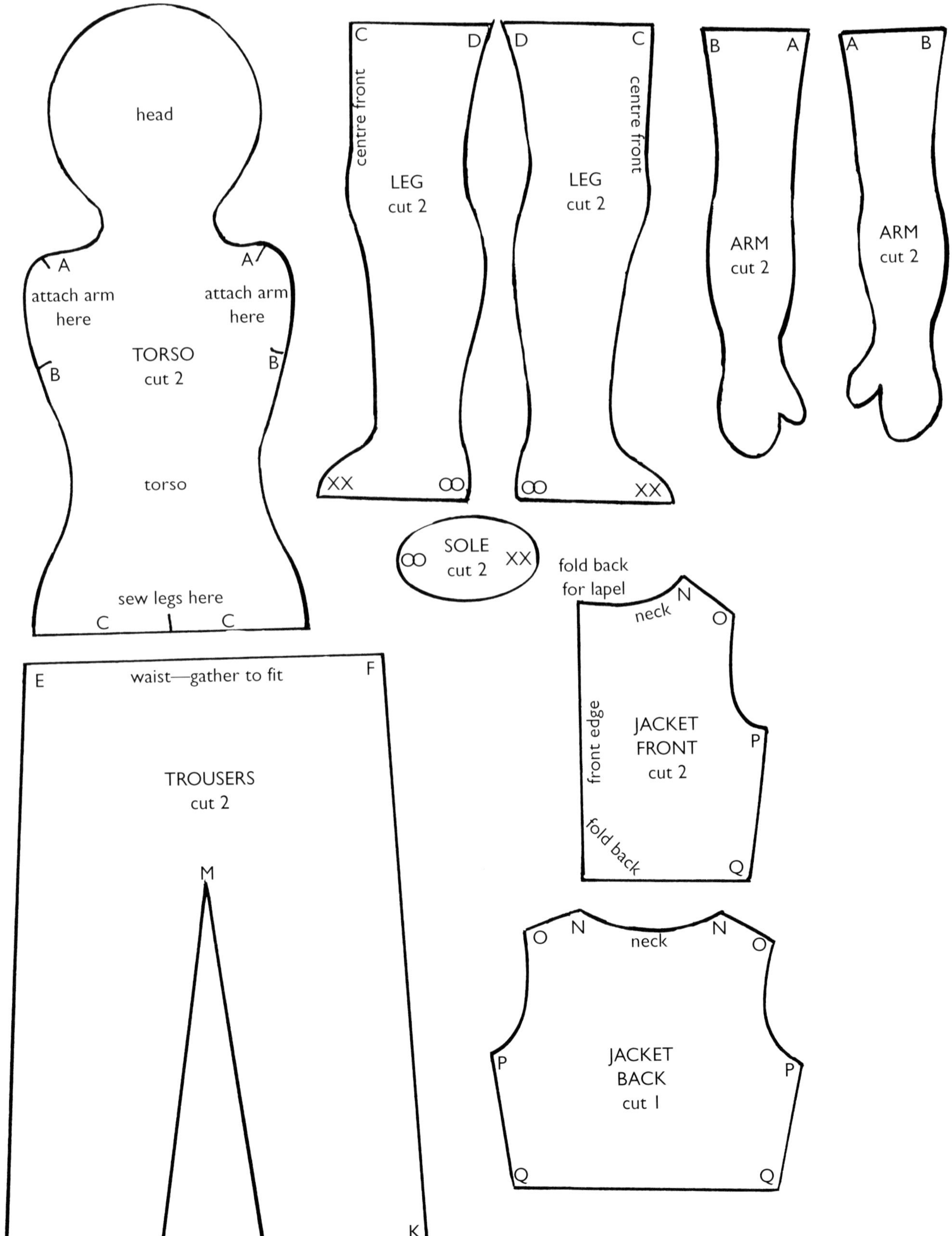

Golly Dazzler pattern layout

Actual Size

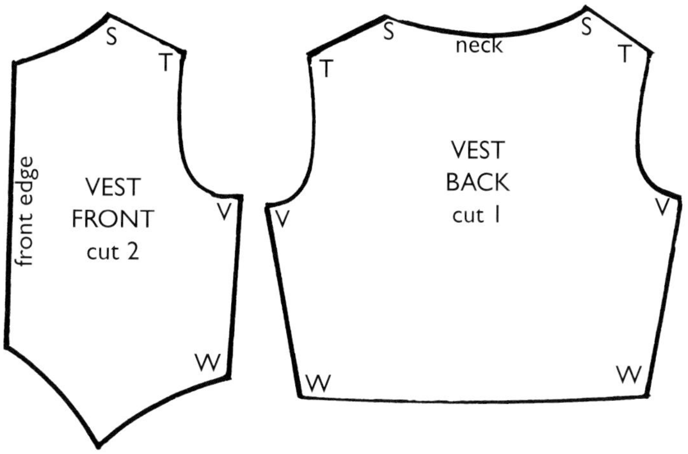

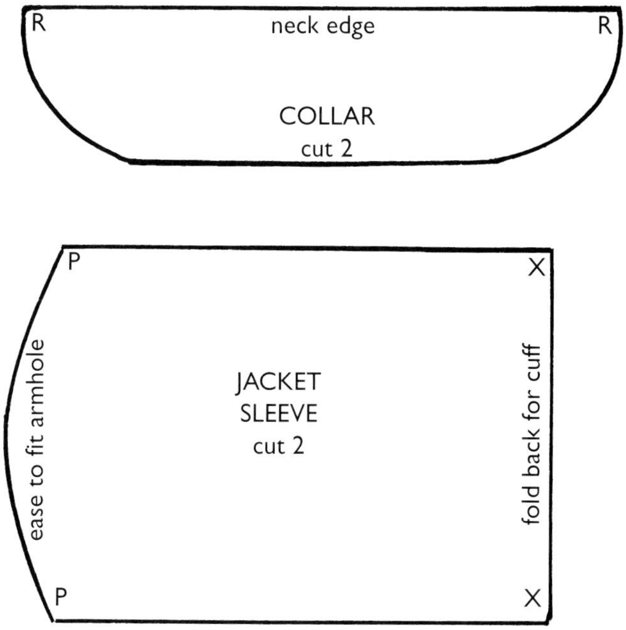

Golly Dazzler pattern layout

Actual Size

If you wish to use glitter as a decoration on the turnback cuffs and bottom of jacket, take jacket off carefully without disturbing cuff turnback, place jacket on a piece of paper, spread a little glue on these areas and sprinkle a generous amount of glitter over the glue. When glue has dried, shake to get rid of any extra glitter and put jacket back on Golly.

Collar

Cut out collar from white felt, and place in position around neck, catching at centre front.
Make a small bow out of ribbon; place at centre front of collar.
Glue gold beads down front of jacket to act as buttons.

Face

Glue a black bead on each sequin, a little below the centre hole of sequin (to avoid a too-starey look), then glue each eye in position with clear-drying craft glue. Make mouth in the shape of your choice out of red felt, and glue in place.

Hair

Take a small piece of black faux fur (long enough to go from ear to ear if Golly had ears), and pin along the head seam, then carefully cut a V shape in the back of the fur so that the hair can be pinned to fit neatly down on the head. When you are satisfied with the shape, carefully glue wig in position.

Crochet Gollies

Golly Gosh

Illustrated on page 49

This small 13.5 cm (5¼") Golly wears trousers with a contrast side stripe. He can be made in an evening, and although I have worked him in 4-ply wool, he can easily be made larger by using thicker denier (ply) wool and a larger crochet hook.

Materials

25 g (1 oz) black 4-ply wool
25 g (1 oz) red 4-ply wool, or colour of your choice, for trousers
25 g (1 oz) green 4-ply wool, or a contrasting colour, for jacket
small ball of white 4-ply wool for the vest, or small piece of white felt
(these amounts will make several Gollies)
2 mm (14) [US B/1] crochet hook
1 large knitting needle 6.5–7.5 cm (3–1) [US 10½–11] to make the curls
small ball of blue wool, or other contrast colour, for the stripe down the leg (optional)
2 white sequins for eyes
2 small black beads for eyes
4 gold sequins for buttons
Note: American readers—work all the dc (double crochet) instructions as sc (single crochet).

Tension

7 dc over 2.5 cm (1") width

Trousers (worked sidewise)

Beginning at one front, with red wool, work 16ch, turn, miss 1ch, and work 1dc into each ch to end, turn with 1ch (15dc).
1st row: 15dc, 1ch, turn.
Repeat the last row 4 times. Fasten off but do not cut.

Contrast stripe

Starting at other end of work, work one row of dc in blue. End off and cut.
Return to where you have left the red wool, and work 1st row 5 times.
Next row: 6dc, 10ch (centre back).
Next row: Turn, miss 1ch, 1dc into each of next 9ch, then 1dc in each of next 6dc (15dc).
Using red—repeat 1st row 4 times.
Using blue—work 1 row of dc (end off securely).
Using red—repeat 1st row 5 times.
Starting at waist end, work 6 dc in red. End off (this gives you the centre front seam row).

Jacket

The jacket is worked from waist up, including sleeves.

Jacket tail

With green wool make 2ch, turn.
1st row: Miss 1ch, 2dc in next 1ch, turn.
2nd row: 2 dc in 1st dc, 1dc, 1ch, turn.
3rd row: 1 dc in the first 2 sts, 2dc in last st, 1ch, turn.
Keeping the increases at one side of work only, continue till you have worked a row of 7dc. End off.
Repeat for other jacket tail.
Tack the two jacket tail pieces to the back of trousers—straight edges to the middle, and the top of the sloping edge to the side of the contrast stripe.

Main part of jacket

Starting at front edge of the waist with green wool, work 5dc across the front, 1dc at end of stripe row, then work 12dc across the back, but working 1 st from the jacket tail with corresponding stitch of trousers together as 1dc, work 1dc at end of stripe row, work 5dc, 1ch, turn (12dc).
Next row: 12dc, 1ch, turn.
Repeat the last row 4 times.

Sleeves

Starting at front edge of jacket, work 6dc, 7ch, turn.
Next row: Miss 1ch, 1dc in each next 6ch, 1dc in each of next 6dc, 1ch, turn (12dc).
Work 5 rows of 12dc. End off.

Back of jacket and sleeves

Work 6ch, then join wool to next dc of back, work 12dc, 7ch, turn.

Next row: Miss 1st ch, work 1dc in each next 6ch, work 1dc in each next 12dc, 1dc in each next 6ch, 1ch, turn (24 dc).

Work 5 rows of dc on these 24dc. End off.

Other front sleeve

Return to base of back, 6ch, 1dc in remaining 6dc.

Work 5 rows of 12dc. End off.

Sew up both shoulder seams, leaving 4 sts open at back neck and 2 sts at each front.

Hands

With black wool work 7dc across ends of rows on arm.

Work 3 rows of 7dc. End off.

Repeat for other hand.

Feet

With black wool work 8dc across ends of rows on leg.

Work 2 rows of 8dc. End off.

Repeat for other leg.

Sew up inside leg seams, and up front seam to armhole level.

Vest

With white wool, starting with 3ch, miss 1ch, 2dc.

Next row inc in each dc (4dc).

Next row inc at each end of row (6dc).

Repeat last row once (8 dc).

Work 1 row of 8dc. End off.

Place this piece inside front of jacket, and then turn back the tops of jacket fronts to form lapels. Stitch vest in place. You can substitute a piece of white felt if you wish.

Starting at the feet, stuff Golly firmly, but do not stuff out of shape.

Head

With black wool, work 5ch.

1st row: Miss 1ch, 1dc in each next 4ch, 1 ch, turn (4 dc).

2nd row: 2dc in 1st st, 1dc in next 2 sts, 2dc in last st, 1 ch, turn (6dc).

3rd row: 6dc, 1ch, turn.

Repeat the last row 3 times.

Next row: Work 2dc tog, 2dc, work 2dc tog, 1ch, turn.

Next row: 4 dc. End off.

Make another head piece the same.

Sew up head leaving the 1st row of 4dc open for stuffing. Stuff head.

To make up

Sew head to body, adding any extra stuffing necessary as you go, so that neck area is quite firm.

Curls

Wind the black wool 6 or 7 times around the large knitting needle, then slide a darning needle threaded with black wool through the loops on the knitting needle, and oversew twice. Repeat for as many curls as you wish to make. Sew curls in place on head.

Finishing

Glue one black bead onto each of the white sequins with clear-drying craft glue, then glue in place on front of head. Use red wool to embroider a mouth. Finally glue two gold sequins down the front join to represent buttons, and one gold sequin at each side of back split of coat. Tie a small length of ribbon into a bow and sew at front of neck.

D.C. Golly

Illustrated on page 50

Worked entirely in double crochet using 8-ply wool, this bright and colourful 41 cm (16") Golly has his lovely red and black striped trousers worked slightly differently to normal crochet, but the technique is quite easy to master.

Materials

50 g (2 oz) ball of black 8-ply wool or yarn
50 g (2 oz) ball of red 8-ply
50 g (2 oz) ball of yellow 8-ply
4 mm (8) [US F/5] crochet hook (loose crocheters use a hook one size smaller)
small ball of white 8-ply for collar
strip of black faux fur 5 cm (2") wide for hair
black and white felt for eyes
red felt for mouth
length of bright ribbon for bow
4 gold buttons for decoration
Note: US readers—work all double crochet (dc) instructions as single crochet (sc).

Tension

5 dc over 2.5 cm (1") width

Making the stripes: To achieve a nice striped look without a lot of ending off and darning in of ends, you will often finish a row at one end, and start the next row in another colour at the other end. Thus when I say 'fasten off', I do not mean 'cut the thread', I mean 'thread the ball of wool through the last loop made and pull firmly'. This ends the work off so that it does not unravel and you can work the following row from the other end without fear of your work coming undone.

Trousers

Using red wool and 4 mm (8) [US F/5] crochet hook, make 13ch, turn, miss 1ch, and work 1dc into each ch to end, 1ch, turn (12dc).
Next row: 1dc in each dc, 2dc in last dc. Fasten off.
Using black wool, and starting from opposite end:
Next row: 1dc into each dc, 2dc in last dc, 17ch. Fasten off.
Starting at waist level (straight edge) with red:
Next row: 13dc, then 1dc in each ch (30dc), 1 ch, turn.
Next row: 30dc. Fasten off.
Work 1 row of 30dc in black.
Continuing to work in pattern of 30dc per row, work 2 rows of red, 1 row of black, until 6 full sets of the 3-row pattern have been worked, finishing with a black row. End off black.
Returning to waist edge with red:
Next row: 13dc, 1ch, turn.
Next row: 2dc tog, work 1dc in each st to end of row. End off.
Work another piece to match.
Sew up centre front and centre back seams.

Back tails

With the yellow wool, make 2ch, miss 1ch, 2dc into next st, 1ch, turn.
Next row: 2dc in 1st st, 1dc in each dc to the end of the row, 1ch, turn.
Next row: 1dc in each dc, 1ch, turn.
Repeat the last 2 rows until you work 10dc across row. End off.
Work another tail the same, but do not end off.
Tack the two back tails to the back part of the trousers, with straight edges of tails to the centre, matching the centre back seam of trousers.
Using red work 1 row of dc, working together the 20 sts of the tails in conjunction with the row ends of the trousers, 1ch, turn.

Back and Front (in one)

Next row: 20dc, 1ch, turn.
Repeat the last row 7 times.
Next row: 20dc, 16ch, turn.
Next row: Miss 1ch, 1dc into each of the next 15ch, 1dc in each of next 20dc, 16ch.
Next row: Miss 1ch, 1dc into each of the next 15ch, 35dc, 1ch, turn (50dc).
Next row: 50dc, 1ch, turn.
Repeat the last row 6 times.

Front

Working from back of neck to waist.
Next row: 20dc, 6ch, turn.
Next row: Miss 1ch, 25dc, 1ch, turn.
Work 5 rows of 25dc.
Next row: 11dc, 1ch, turn.
Repeat the last row 7 times.
Return to neck, miss 10dc, 1dc on next 20dc, 1ch, turn.
Next row: 20dc, 6ch.
Next row: Miss 1ch, 25dc.
Work another piece to match.

Hands

Join in black to end of arms, and work 12dc evenly along row ends, 1ch, turn.
Next row: 5dc, 2dc tog, 5dc (11dc).
Next row: 2dc tog, 7dc, 2dc tog (9dc).
Next row: 3dc, 3dc tog, 3dc (7dc). End off.
Repeat for other hand.

Feet

With black work 18dc evenly around row ends of trousers.
Next row: 2dc tog, 6dc, 2dc tog, 6dc, 2dc tog (15dc).
Next row: 2dc tog, work to last 2dc, 2dc tog (13dc).
Next row: 2dc tog, 4dc, 2dc tog, 4dc, 2dc tog. End off.

Head

With black wool work 11ch.
1st row: Miss 1ch, 1dc into each ch to end, 1ch, turn (10dc).
2nd row: 2dc into 1st dc, 8dc, 2dc into last dc, 1ch, turn (12dc).
3rd row: 12dc, 1ch, turn.
4th row: 2dc in 1st dc, 10dc, 2dc in last dc, 1ch, turn (14 dc).
5th row: 14dc, 1ch, turn.
6th row: 2dc in 1st dc, 12dc, 2dc in last st, 1ch, turn (16dc).
Work 6 rows on these 16dc without shaping.
Next row: 2dc tog, 12dc, 2dc tog (14dc).
Next row: 2dc tog, work in dc to last 2 st, 2dc tog.
Continue to decrease at both ends of every row until 8dc. End off.

Collar

With white work 25ch.
Next row: Miss 1ch, 1dc into each st to end (24dc), 1ch, turn.
Next row: 24dc, 1ch, turn.
Next row: 2dc in 1st st, 6dc, 2dc in next dc, 8dc, 2dc in next dc, 6dc, 2dc in last st.
Next row: 2dc in 1st dc, 8dc, 2dc in next dc, 8dc, 2dc in next dc, 8dc, 2dc in last st.
Next row: 2dc in 1st dc, 1dc in each st to last st, 2dc.

Belt

With black wool work 22ch loosely.
Miss 1ch, work 21dc. End. off.

To make up

Sew up inside leg seams, and bottoms of feet. Sew up front seam and side seams of jacket, leaving open at neck. Sew the front of the jacket to the front of the pants. Stuff body firmly. Sew up head seam leaving open at neck. Stuff head firmly.

Attach head to body, adding extra stuffing in neck area if necessary, to give a firm join.

Sew collar around neck to hide neck join, and stitch collar together at front. Sew bow in place, and add buttons down centre front, and one each side of centre back split. With belt level with waist anchor at both side seams.

Using clear-drying glue, glue the black eye parts to the white eye parts, then glue the eyes to the head. Glue mouth in place on head.

Above: GOLLY GEE SLIPPER FACES are just the thing to set young feet dancing across the room. The basic heads can easily be made small enough to go on a toddler's slippers (page 68)

Above: BABY'S BIB A band of Gollies worked in cross-stitch marches across baby's bib. You could also work them back-to-back or face-to-face in pairs (page 67)

Left: TEACOSY GOLLY These happy Gollies will keep your favourite teapots nice and cosy. Quick to crochet, the large size worked in 8-ply, the smaller size in 5-ply (page 65)

ABOVE: KNITTED HAND PUPPET This cheerful fellow, worked in 8-ply, is waiting his turn in the wings (page 72)

ABOVE: SCRAP-BAG WALLHANGING Children love this happy, quick to make wallhanging. It is also a fun way of teaching a beginner the elements of machine sewing (page 74)

LEFT: SEWN HAND PUPPET My six year old grandson Jefferson, following in the family tradition of puppeteering, is having lots of fun seeing what this sewn puppet can do (page 70)

Gollies Galore

ıaking a small woollen toy. It will cause
.member making one of these when I was
ns. I have taken the old idea several steps
and dressing him in the traditional way. Be-
a workshop teaching him to what started out as
ıich grew to 40 (all that could possibly fit in the
.ntion in Anaheim, California, where we all had a
he simple design of this Golly is also ideal for a school
.ıior citizens group. I hope you have as much fun making
ıesigning and teaching of him. My husband Jim did the
ĸe life easier for those who have never used this technique.

ply knitting wool or yarn
bouclé or similar knotted yarn (for hair)
ɩrong cardboard 10 cm (4") wide
ɾ strong cardboard 6.5 cm (2½") wide
ˌuare of felt in the colour chosen for trousers
square of felt in the colour chosen for jacket
(these quantities are sufficient for several Gollies)
scrap of contrast colour or white felt for vest
scrap of contrast colour felt or ribbon for bow tie
2 white sequins
2 small black beads
red wool or small piece of red felt for mouth
small gold or coloured beads for buttons

To make the Woolly Golly follow the simple instructions and drawings from Figure 1 to Figure 6.

Clothes

Using the patterns on page 64 cut out the two pants pieces, the vest, and the one-piece coat.

1. Take the two leg pieces and sew the side seams (AB and CD) by using an oversew or back stitch. You can glue the seams with a clear-drying craft glue if you wish, but sewing gives a better finish.
2. Sew the inside of legs (E–F–G). Turn right side out. Put trousers on Golly, carefully pushing each leg in turn into his trousers. Run a gathering thread around waist to fit. End off securely.
3. Glue the vest into position at the front, with the tags over the shoulder and the points of the vest over the pants.
4. Fold the coat pieces so that H and J meet and L and M meet. Sew from H to J and then from L to M. Turn coat right side out. Place on Golly, carefully putting arms into sleeves.

To finish

Turn back lapels P to suit, and glue in place. If necessary, stitch across shoulder seams on each side. If you wish you can also turn back R on each side.

Place bow of felt or ribbon in place at neck, then you can decorate with beads, giving Golly buttons down his vest, on the front of his coat, with two at the top of the slit at back of the coat.

If you are really enthusiastic you can sew or glue a contrast seam down the side of each trouser leg, and use glitter on his lapels as one of my students in Anaheim did—the Golly looked marvellous.

Face

This gives Golly his character. Take two white sequins and glue a black bead in place in each sequin, glue the eyes into position on the Golly's face. Either work a mouth using red wool, or cut out a smiling or singing mouth from red felt and glue into position.

If you wish you can sew or glue a brooch (pin) catch on the back of your Golly, so you can wear him, or you can use Golly as an accessory for your favourite doll or bear.

Figure 1

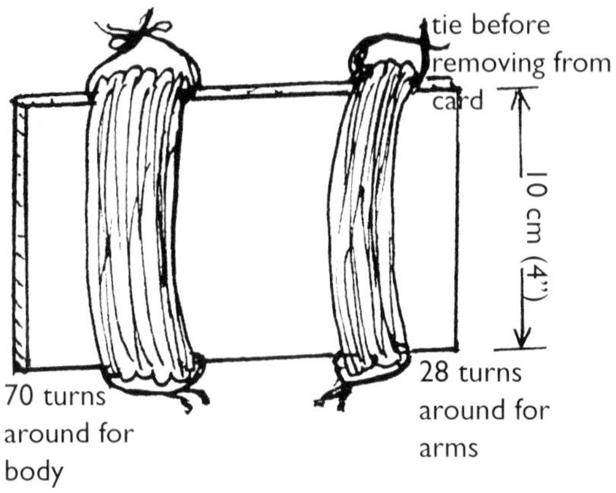

Figure 2

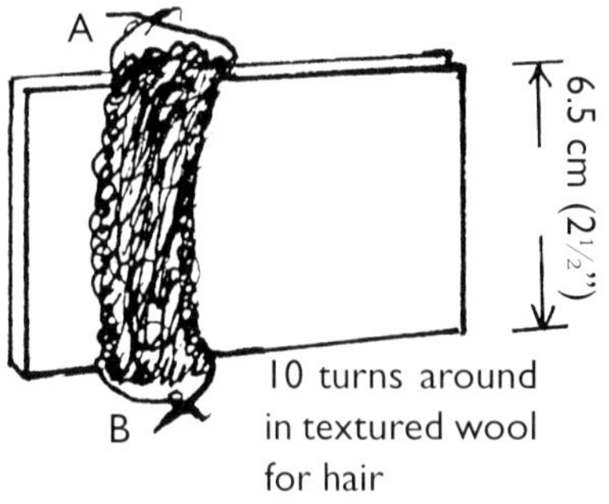

Figure 3

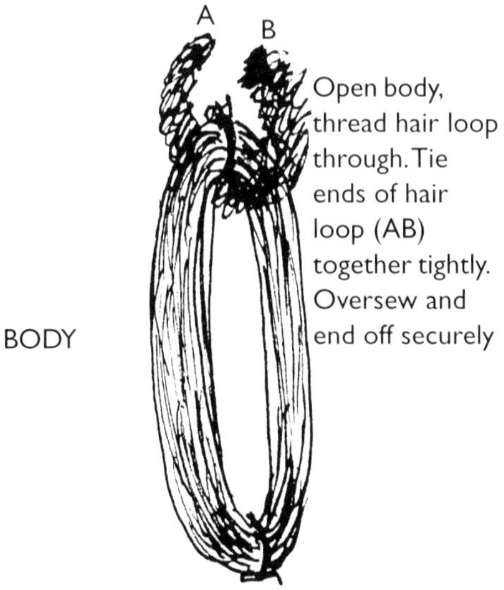

Figure 4

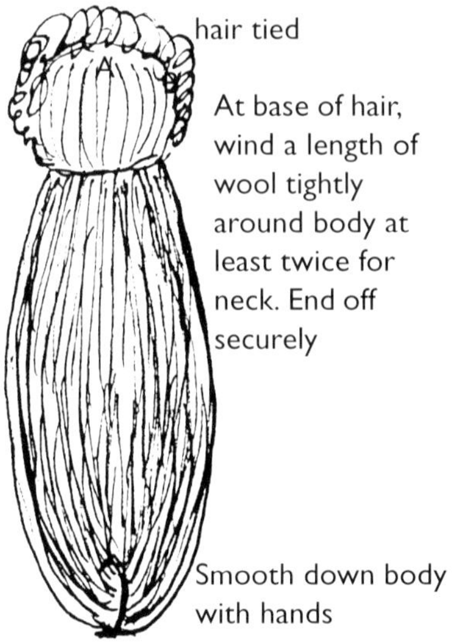

Figure 5

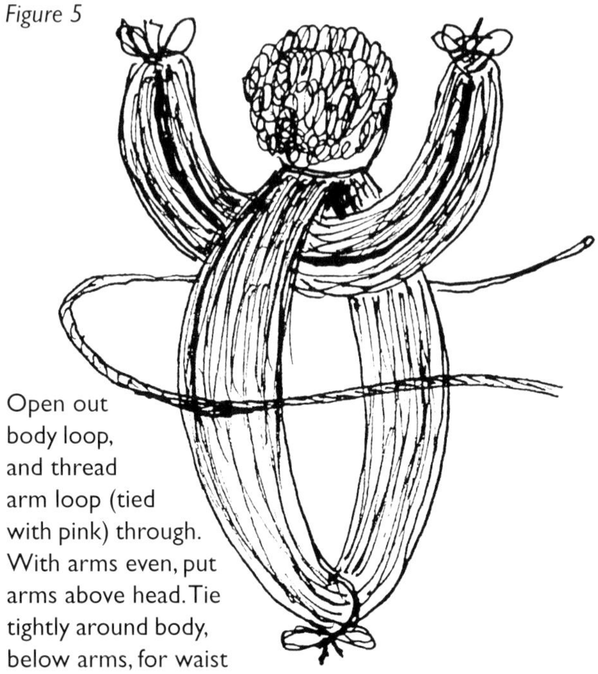

Figure 6

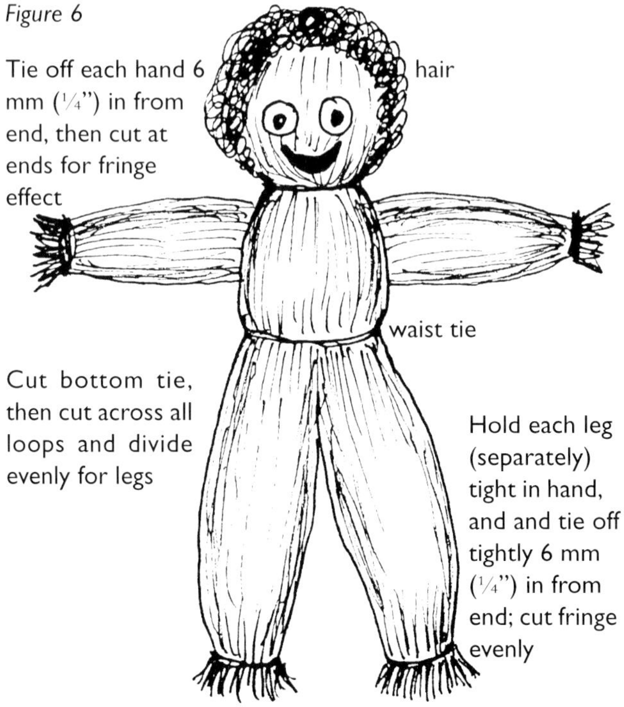

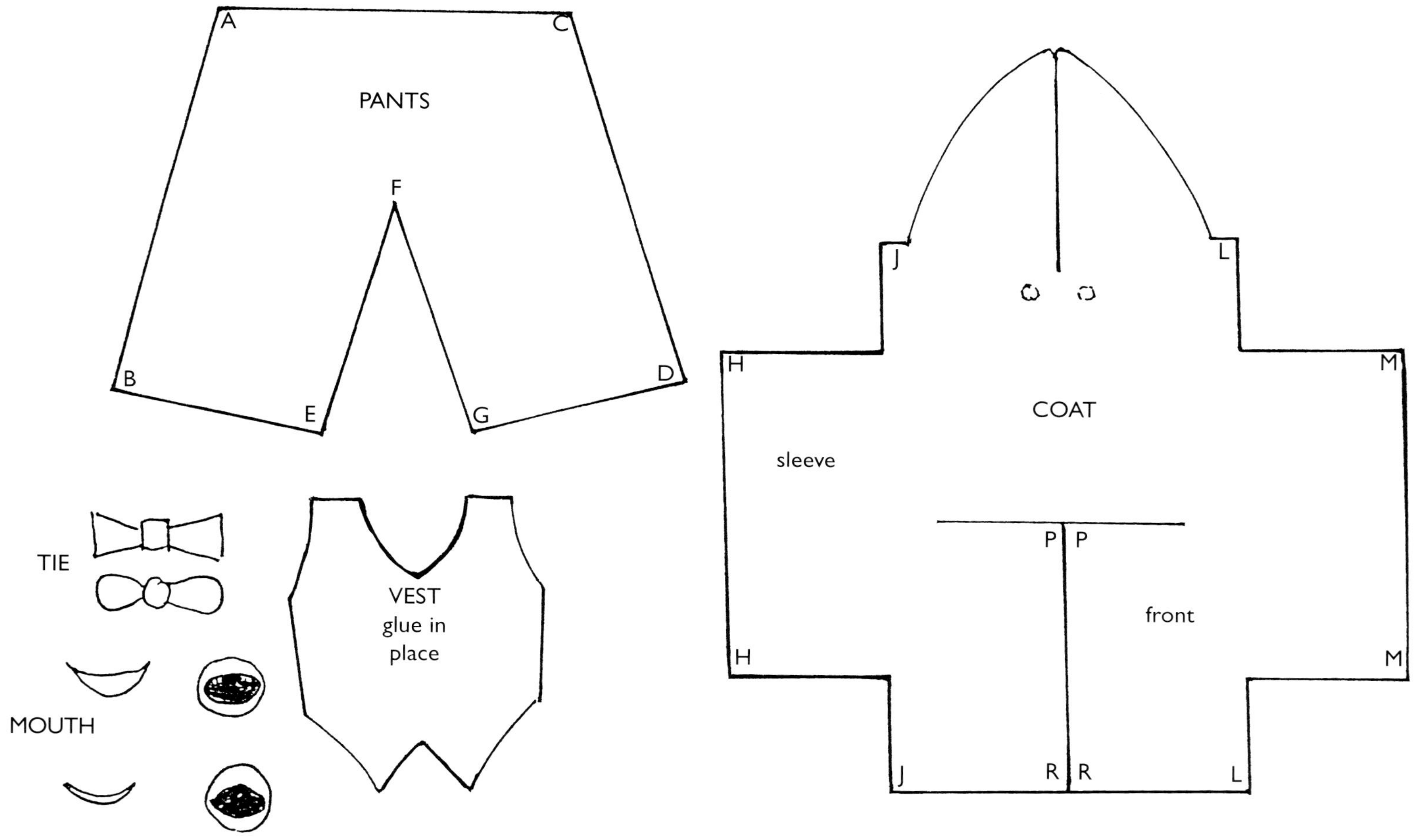

Woolly Golly pattern layout

Actual Size

Teacosy Golly

Illustrated on page 59

This happy smiling fellow in crochet will brighten up your mornings, be a talking point for visitors, maybe an ideal gift to lighten the day for a favourite relative or friend. Worked entirely in double crochet (US single crochet) he is quick and easy to make; by selecting different ply wool and different sized crochet hooks, the teacosy can be made to fit most teapots. The teacosy worked in 8-ply will easily fit a 6–8 cup teapot. The cosy can easily be made smaller by working fewer rows.

Materials

50 g (2 oz) ball of red 8-ply wool
25 g (1 oz) of yellow 8-ply wool
50 g (2 oz) of black 8-ply wool
25 g (1 oz) blue 8-ply wool
3.00 mm (11) [US D] crochet hook
small quantity of stuffing for the head
2 large plastic googly eyes, or leftover scraps of black and white felt for eyes
small piece of red felt or velvet for the mouth
20 cm (8") of felt for lining if thought necessary

Note: US readers—work all dc (double crochet) instructions as sc (single crochet); work all tr (treble) instructions as dc (double crochet).

Tension

8 ply—5 dc over 2.5 cm (1") width
5 ply—7 dcs over 2.5 cm (1") width

Front

Side front and arm

With red wool, and 3 mm (11) [US D] hook make 25ch.
1st row: Miss 1ch, work 1dc into each of the next 24ch, 1ch, turn (24dc).
2nd row: 2dc into 1st dc, 1dc into each dc to the end of the row (25dc).
3rd row: 1dc in each dc to last dc, 2dc, 1ch, turn (26dc).
Repeat 2nd and 3rd rows 3 times.
10th row: Work as per 2nd row (33dc).
11th row: Work 9dc (in red). Fasten off. Join in black wool and work next 24dc in black. Fasten off.
Return to shaped end of work.
12th row: Using red wool, work 1ch, 33dc, 1ch, turn.
13th row: 33dc, 1ch, turn.
Repeat 13th row 8 times. Fasten off.

Vest

Join in yellow and work 12 rows of 33dc, making 1ch turn in each row. Fasten off yellow.

Side front and arm

Work 10 rows of 33dc in red.
Next row: Working from the top of the work (shaped side) work 9dc in red, 24dc in black. Fasten off.
Next row: Join in red wool at shaped side and work as follows:
* *1st row:* Work the first 2dc tog, 1dc in each dc to end, 1ch, turn (32dc).
2nd row: 1dc into each dc to last 2dc, work 2dc tog, 1ch, turn (31dc).
Repeat the last two rows 3 times (25dc).
Next row: Work the 1st row again.
Next row: 24dc. Fasten off.*

Back

Using red wool only, work the first 10 rows as front.
Work 44 rows of 33dc, 1ch, turn.
Work from * to * for next 10 rows. Fasten off.
Sew up both sides 25 mm (1") from bottom.

Trousers

With blue wool, work 1dc into end of each row, right around bottom of teapot, sl st to join.
Next 2 rows: 1ch, then 1dc in each dc, sl st to join. Fasten off.
If you are making the cosy for a tall teapot or large coffee-pot work more rounds in blue.

Head (make 2)

Make 3ch, and form into a ring.
1st round: 3ch, 11tr, sl st to top of 3ch to join (12tr).
2nd round: 3ch, 1tr into same place, 2tr into each tr in previous round, sl st to top of 3ch (24 tr).
3rd round: 3ch, 1tr into same place, 1tr into next tr; then *2tr into next tr, 1tr into next tr, repeat from * to end, sl st into top of 3ch to join (36tr).
4th round: 3ch, 1tr into same place, 1tr into each of the next 2tr, *2tr into next tr, 1tr into each of next 2tr, repeat from * to end, sl st to join.
5th round: 3ch, 1tr into same place, 1tr into each of the next 3tr, *2tr into next tr, 1tr into each of the next 3tr, repeat from * to end, sl st to join. Fasten off.

Bow

With blue wool, work 9ch.
Next row: Miss 1ch, 8dc, 1ch, turn.
Work 29 rows of 8dc, using 1ch to turn. Fasten off.

Bow strap

With blue wool, work 3ch.
Next row: Miss 1ch, 2dc, 1ch, turn.
Work 11 rows of 2dc, turning with ch.
Sew the two short ends of the bow together, fold with join at centre back, then place bow strap around middle of bow, and sew in position at back of bow.

To make up

If you wish, line both pieces of body carefully with felt, but as the crochet is closely worked, lining may not be necessary.

Sew up top edge, and gather in slightly to fit teapot. Sew up one side to suit position of spout and on the other side leave a wider opening for handle.

Sew together both pieces of head, leaving an opening the width of the centre piece or vest. Stuff head lightly, then sew across opening, and join to top of vest, matching back of head to back of teacosy.

Hair

Wind a quantity of black wool around a strong piece of cardboard or thin plywood 5 cm (2") wide. Cut windings along one side of wood only, and put cut pieces together. Take 2 lengths of wool at a time and fold in half. Place crochet hook through a tr st 2.5 cm (1") from where head has been joined to body, place folded wool over hook, draw through, and then draw loose ends through loop to knot threads off. Continue around the head in this manner to other side, finishing 2.5 cm (1") from where the head joins body. Clip Golly's hair so it is all the same length.

Face

Using either white and black felt to form the eyes, or plastic sew-on googly eyes, position eyes and glue or sew in place. Make a mouth out of red felt or velvet, sew or glue in place with clear-drying craft glue.

Sew bow in position at top of vest, and if you wish sew a couple of flat gold buttons down front of vest.

All you need now is some tea, hot water, milk if you like it, a slice of cake or a biscuit, and a friend to share a 'cuppa' with.

Baby's bib

Illustrated on page 59

Large towelling baby bibs with bands of Aida cloth for embroidery are available in most good craft shops or even large supermarkets or department stores. Having just been blessed with a new grandchild, I thought of a lovely way to decorate such a bib and designed a simple Golly in cross-stitch. The actual Golly is a repeat of 16 squares, with as many squares as you wish between repeats to make a border.
The design can also be used on a guest towel for a young visitor, or so that a child easily recognises their own special towel at day-care or kindergarten.
Worked in the traditional blue and red Golly colours (although he can be embroidered in any colours you want), this Golly has a lovely golden-yellow bow at the neck, a white vest and even, if you look closely, a red mouth.

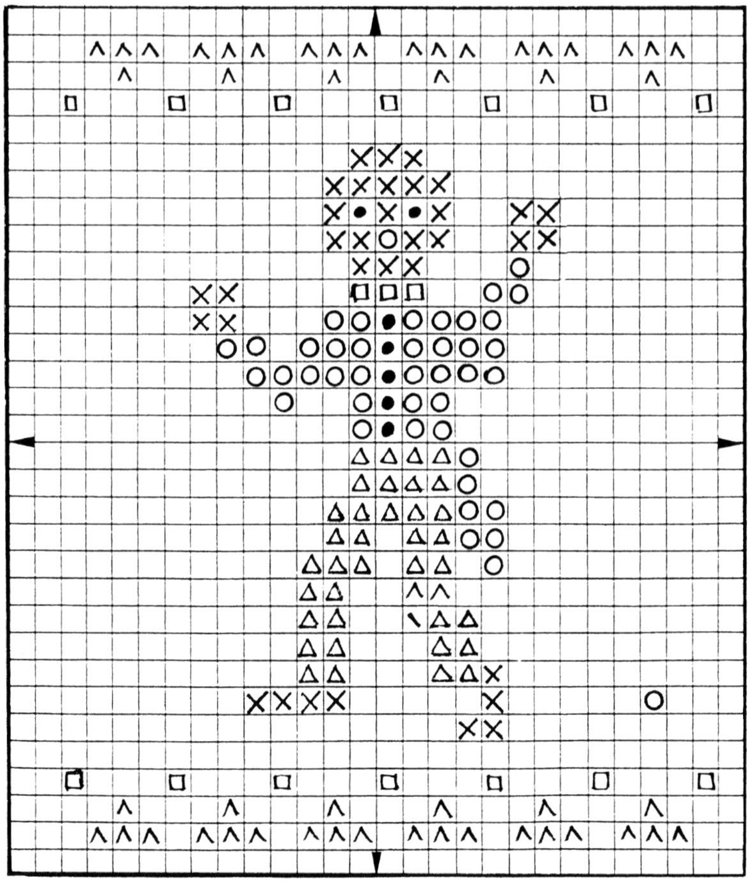

- • white
- ☒ black
- ◻ gold
- ○ red
- △ blue
- ∧ green
- ⟍ half cross, blue

DMC or Anchor stranded cotton, work using 3 strands

Golly Gee slipper faces

Illustrated on page 59

I designed these fun faces for my teenage grand-daughters, who love something a bit unusual. They can be added to a pair of slippers or even to denim shoes to raise a laugh amongst the younger (or older but young-at-heart) set, and can become quite a talking point to enliven any get-together. Simple to make, each face is only two pieces with a length of fur sewn in as you go, with the features and essential bow added afterwards.

Materials

10 cm (4") black cotton fabric (I used velvet but any strong black cotton fabric can be used)
2 x 20 cm x 5 cm (8" x 2") strips medium length black faux fur
4 plastic sew-on or glue-on googly eyes or scraps of black and white felt
scrap of red felt for mouth
square of yellow felt for bow
Dacron for stuffing (firm offcuts)

Face

Fold the two strips of fur lengthwise, with right sides out, pin or baste edges, then sew (using zig-zag or overlocking stitch) along the edge of the fur, keeping strands of fur away from edge.

Mark the middle of each fur piece at the sewn edge.

Cut four pieces of fabric in the face shape. If using velvet or other napped fabric, keep the nap smoothed downwards.

Fold each face piece in half and mark top and the bottom with cotton or special white marking pencil.

With right side of one face piece facing you, match the top middle mark of the face piece to the middle edge marking of the fur. Pin. Gently ease the fur down each side of the head from the middle, pinning as you go, checking that the ends are equidistant from the bottom head marking when finished. Tack in place.

Sew the fur to the head piece, stroking the fur away from the edge as you go.

Take another face piece, and with the right sides together, match the top markings to the face with fur attached. Pin pieces together.

Care must be taken with the next step to achieve the best results.

Working from the top, carefully pin down each side of the head, stroking the fur as you go so that it lies straight inside the enclosed piece (pointing towards the centre). Tack, then sew around head with the machine, leaving the space between the ends of the fur open.

Turn face right side out, and stuff firmly, keeping a rather flattish appearance.

Sew up the opening with ladder stitch or oversew.

Repeat to make other face for the second slipper.

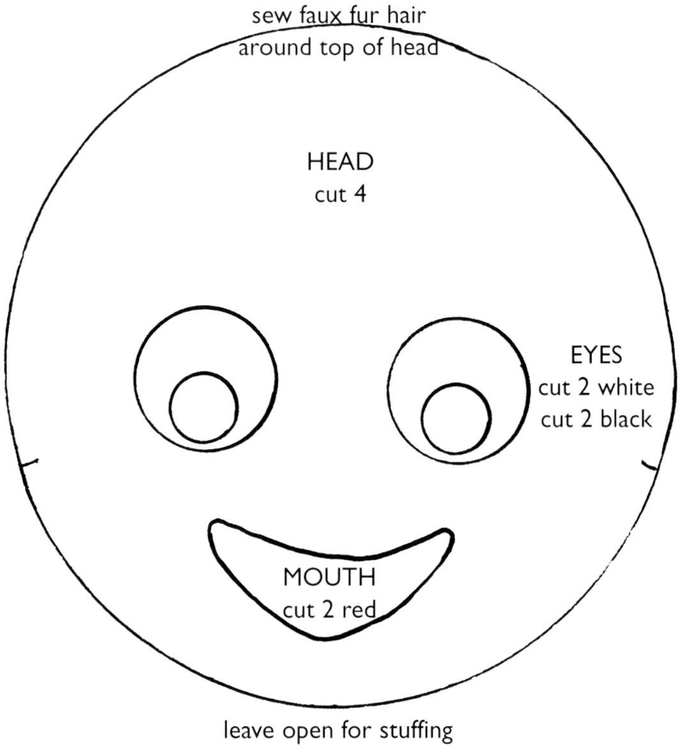

Bow

Cut a piece of felt 15 cm x 4 cm (6" x 1½"), fold in half and mark the centre of both long edges. Sew the two short edges together, then match the sewn edge with the centre marks (forming the bow). Gather across this middle section through both thicknesses several times, pulling tightly. Cut a strip of matching felt 1 cm (3/8") wide, or contrasting fabric 2.5 cm (1") wide folded and glued in half, and wrap this strip around centre of bow, stitching at the back.

Stitch the bow securely into position at the base of the face on the section which was oversewn after stuffing.

Repeat on other face.

Attach the white and black felt eyes and red felt mouth by stitching or using clear-drying craft glue to give your Golly faces their character.

Finishing

Place the faces on the slippers or shoes and sew in position at the top and sides. If you find it hard to sew the bottom section of the face to the shoe or slipper, use glue. For extra security sew down or glue the back of the bow as well.

Sewn hand puppet

Illustrated on page 60

Children fortunate enough to have a glove puppet can enter a realm of imagination and make-believe where they can express themselves through the puppet and its actions. I hope the children you make this Golly puppet for have hours of fun with their new companion.

Materials

30 cm (12") black velvet or felt (I used velvet but a strong cotton could be substituted)
small scrap of white poplin or gaberdine for the collar, hands and eyes
scrap of black felt for eyes
scrap of red felt for mouth
length of fancy ribbon for bow tie
length of black faux fur 5 cm (2") wide for hair
10 cm x 5 cm (4" x 2") buckram or other stiffened fabric

Method

Cut out two body pieces, two head pieces, four hand pieces and collar from the patterns.

Sew up shoulder seams. Sew up the shaped side of each hand. Sew the hands to the ends of the sleeves.

With wrong side of work facing you, finish sewing around hands and down both side seams. Make a small hem at the bottom of the Golly body.

If you wish you can stuff the hands to give them a fuller effect (this is a good idea if the puppet is for a young child).

Make the tube of buckram or stiffened fabric following the diagram.

Join the two halves of the head together, leaving the neck section open. Turn right side out, and stuff the top part of the head before inserting the tube of buckram. Gently stuff each side of the tube, making sure that your finger can still go up into the head. Sew head to tube, leaving a small portion of the buckram tube free to slip into the body.

Sew head to body, catching buckram at the same time. This gives a strong join.

Fold faux fur in half, sew along the long edge. Pin hair in position around the head seam. Sew in place, sewing first from the front and then from the back. Cut out two long white eye pieces, and two black pupils. Glue the white eye pieces in place, then position the black pupils to give the expression you are aiming for, and glue in place. Cut the mouth out of red felt and glue in place.

Put collar in position. Turning the collar up towards the hair, stitch in place around the neck and then fold the collar back over the stitching to give the right effect. Finish with a fancy bow, and let Golly do his act.

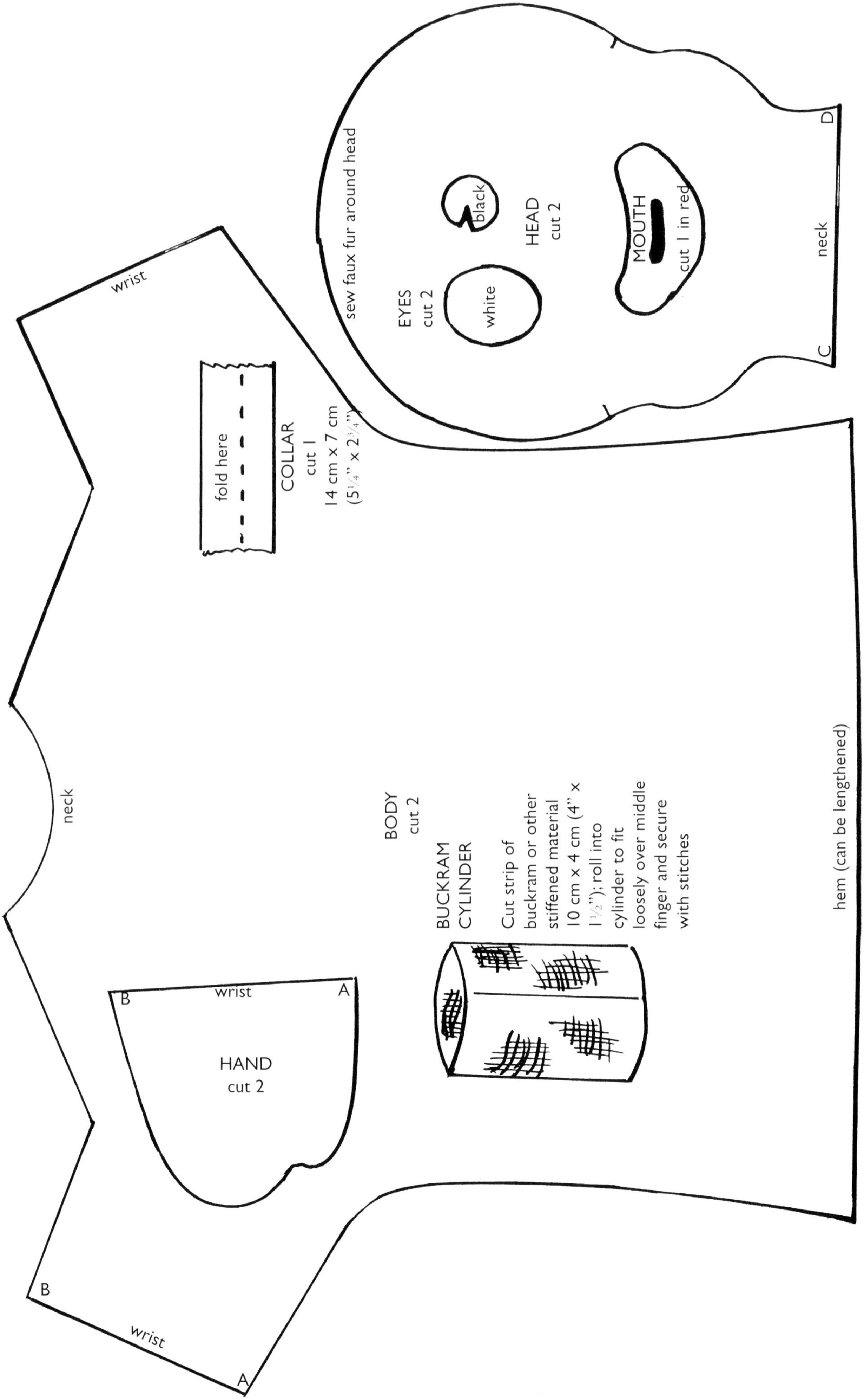
sew faux fur around head
EYES
cut 2
white
black
HEAD
cut 2
MOUTH
cut 1 in red
neck
C
D
wrist
fold here
COLLAR
cut 1
14 cm x 7 cm
(5¼" x 2¾")
neck
BODY
cut 2
BUCKRAM
CYLINDER
Cut strip of
buckram or other
stiffened material
10 cm x 4 cm (4" x
1½"); roll into
cylinder to fit
loosely over middle
finger and secure
with stitches
hem (can be lengthened)
wrist
B
A
HAND
cut 2
B
wrist
A

Knitted hand puppet

Illustrated on page 60

Having been at one time a professional puppeteer, I know the enjoyment children get not only from watching puppets perform, but also from manipulating them. I still remember the pleasure I derived from the monkey glove puppet I was given as a child, which was unfortunately discarded through becoming rather moth-eaten. This simply knitted Golly is just the right size and form for a child to enjoy.

Materials

50 g (2 oz) 8-ply black wool or yarn
25 g (1 oz) red or contrast 8-ply wool or yarn for the lapels
pair of 3 mm (11) [US 3] knitting needles
1 square of white felt for vest and cuffs
length of black faux fur for hair
10 cm x 5 cm (4" x 2") buckram or other stiffened fabric
2 plastic googly eyes
scrap of red felt for mouth
length of coloured ribbon for bow tie

Tension

7 sts over 2.5 cm (1") width.

Body and arms

With 8-ply black wool and 3 mm (11) [US 3] needles cast on 36 sts and work 42 rows in st st.
Next row: Inc 1 st at each end of the row.
Next row: Purl.
Repeat these 2 rows twice.
Cast on 10 sts at beg of next 2 rows (beginning of the arms).
Work 8 rows in st st.
Divide for neck opening as follows:
Next row: k26, cast off 10 sts, k26.
Working on the last 26 sts:
*Dec 1 st at the neck edge only on the next 5 rows.
Next row: Knit.
Inc 1 st at neck edge on next 5 rows (26 sts)*. Leave these sts on a safety holder.
Join the wool to the neck edge of first sts and then work from * to *.
Next row: k26, cast on 10 sts, then knit the 26 sts from the safety holder (62 sts).
Work 9 rows in st st.
Cast off 10 sts at beg of next 2 rows.
Dec 1 st at each end of next and following alternate rows twice (36 sts).
Work 42 rows in st st. Cast off.

Head

Cast on 16 sts and work 2 rows.
Inc 1 st at each end of the next and following alternate row (20 sts).
Starting with a purl row, work 19 rows of st st without shaping.
Dec 1 st at each end of next and following alternate row. Cast off.
Make another piece the same.

Neck

Cast on 10 sts and work 24 rows in st st.

Lapels

With red wool and 3 mm (11) [US 3] knitting needles cast on 2 sts.
1st row: k1, p1.
2nd row: p1, k1.
3rd row: k1, p1, inc in last st.
Continue in moss st, inc at end of every 4th row until 10 sts are on needle.
Work 2 rows in m st.
Next row: Cast off 6 sts, m st 4.
Next row: m st 4, cast on 7 sts.
Next row: m st, working into the back of the first 7 sts.
Next row: m st 19, work 2 tog.
Working in m st, dec at the end of every 4th row until 7 sts remain.
Work 8 rows in m st. Cast off.
Work another lapel the same.

To make up

Join side and arm seams, and also arm edge, leaving opening at neck. Stuff arms for the first 2 cm (¾") Using black wool run two rows of gathering stitch around at this point, holding in the stuffing and thus making a hand. End off securely.

Join two head pieces together leaving cast-on stitches open. Stuff head.

Make the piece of buckram or stiffened fabric into a cylinder and glue or stitch so that it slips easily up and down on your first finger.

Join the neck piece into a cylinder and stitch firmly in place about halfway up the cylinder of buckram.

Gather bottom of head slightly and sew firmly to top of neck.

Gather opening of main body, and then sew to bottom of neck, anchoring firmly to buckram. Part of the cylinder thus goes up inside the head, and part into the body of the puppet.

Sew a piece of white felt around the gathers of each arm to form white cuffs.

Cut the faux fur 5 cm (2") wide and long enough to go from where the puppet's ear would be on one side to the same spot on the other side. Fold the fur in half, pin and sew up the long side edge on the machine. With front of puppet facing you, attach the length of fur around the head following the join seam, sewing first to the face side and then the back of the head side.

Sew or glue on the plastic googly eyes.

Glue on a red felt mouth.

Join up the 7 st back seam of the lapels. Pin the two lapels in position on the front of the puppet, crossing them over slightly at the bottom.

Before sewing in place, cut a piece of white felt to fit under the lapels to form a vest. Tack the vest in place. Sew down both the front and outer edges of the lapels. The back part can be left free to give added movement.

Finally make a bow tie from the ribbon and attach at base of the neck. Golly is ready for his first puppet performance.

Scrap-bag wall hanging

Illustrated on page 60

Some months back my daughter-in-law Beth became interested in the Golly I was then knitting, and asked was there any way that she might be able to help, as she loves simple craftwork.
We got talking and she said, 'Why not a wall hanging for a children's room—but I can't draw.'
So I made her a simple sketch pattern. A week later she had made this delightful appliqué wallhanging from bits of fabric from her scrap-bag—and brought it to show me.
It was so simply done that anyone who has a sewing machine able to do the zig-zag stitch can make one in a few hours, with just a little care. A more advanced sewer may like to take the idea and embellish it.

Materials

69 cm x 46 cm (27" x 18") calico or other fabric for backing—this can be smaller or larger
scrap of black velveteen or other black fabric for head, hands and feet
scrap of red or other colour poplin for jacket and mouth
scrap of check cotton fabric in any colour for pants
small piece of white fabric for vest
2 plastic googly eyes
2 black buttons
30 cm (12") ribbon for the bow tie
wooden dowel and a length of cord on which to hang your finished product

Note: All the pattern pieces are shown here at half actual size. Enlarge at 200 per cent (or whatever percentage you choose) by photocopying.

Method

1. Hem sides of calico. Make wider hems at top and bottom. The top hem must be large enough to pass the piece of wooden dowel through.
2. Cut out all the pattern pieces and pin in position on the calico. The jacket goes over the trousers at the dotted line.
3. The hands are pinned over the bottom sleeve at the dotted line, and then the shoes are pinned over the bottom of the trousers at the bottom line.
4. Pin the vest in position at the dotted neckline, and then pin the head over the top edge of the vest.
5. Run tacking or basting stitches around the whole Golly.
6. Using the appropriate colour thread for each piece, zig-zag stitch around Golly.
7. Hair: Cut 12-ply wool into 8 cm (3") lengths, fold each length in half, and sew across just above the folded end. Place hair around head.
8. Sew eyes and mouth in place, and buttons to front of jacket.
9. Cut an 18 cm (7") length of ribbon, fold so that the cut ends are at centre back. Stitch the cut ends. Run a gathering stitch through both thicknesses of ribbon at the centre, and draw up. Cut a piece or ribbon long enough to go round centre gathers and fold in half, and sew this narrow band in place at back of the bow. Stitch the bow in place at the bottom of the head.
10. Slide the dowel in place and tie the length of cord to each end of the dowel.

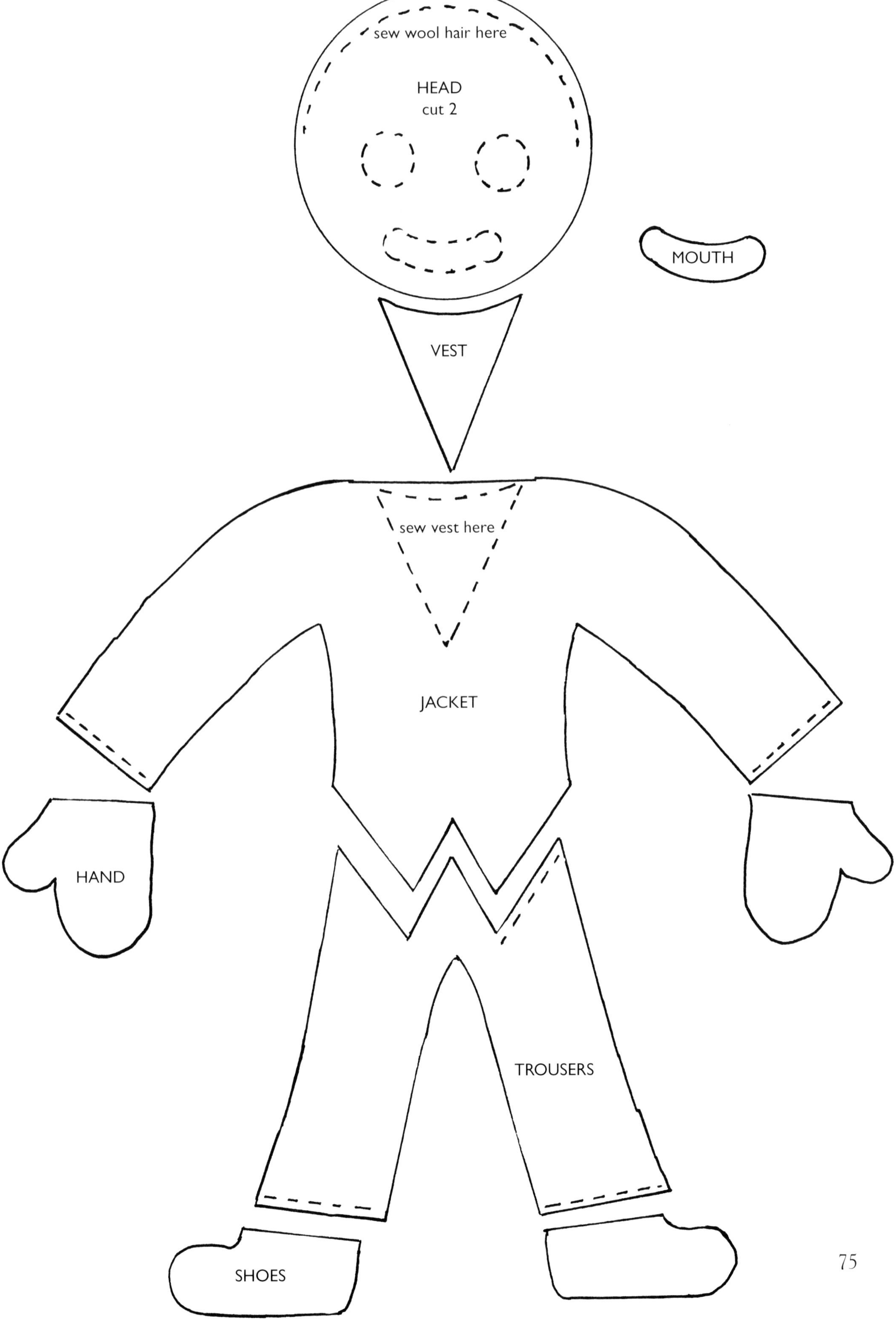
sew wool hair here
HEAD
cut 2
MOUTH
VEST
sew vest here
JACKET
HAND
TROUSERS
SHOES

Index